Everything Old is New Again

Everything Old is New Again

How Entrepreneurs Use Discourse Themes to Reclaim Abandoned Urban Spaces

Miriam Plavin-Masterman

BEP BUSINESS EXPERT PRESS

Everything Old is New Again: How Entrepreneurs Use Discourse Themes to Reclaim Abandoned Urban Spaces

First published in 2018 by
Business Expert Press, LLC
222 East 46th Street, New York, NY 10017
www.businessexpertpress.com

ISBN-13: 978-1-63157-954-7 (paperback)
ISBN-13: 978-1-63157-955-4 (e-book)

Business Expert Press Service Systems and Innovations in Business and Society Collection

Collection ISSN: 2326-2664 (print)
Collection ISSN: 2326-2699 (electronic)

Cover and interior design by Exeter Premedia Services Private Ltd., Chennai, India

First edition: 2018

10 9 8 7 6 5 4 3 2 1

Printed in the United States of America.

Abstract

Canonical entrepreneurship scholars (Schumpeter, Hayek, and others) have argued that entrepreneurial innovation and initiative is a critical part of "creative destruction"—the sometimes difficult process of building social arrangements that challenge and topple existing, less capable predecessors. Although the revitalizing potential of entrepreneurship has often been studied in the context of commercial start-up businesses, recent scholarship on institutional entrepreneurship highlights the kinship between for-profit entrepreneurship and the equally transformative innovation and initiative of entrepreneurs in the nonprofit, community, and policy-activist fields.

This expanded exploration of entrepreneurial potential has become important in the creative destruction—or, more accurately, "creative reclamation"—of abandoned or under-used industrial relics and urban space. My project uses case studies in New York, Chicago, and Philadelphia, where community groups have deployed or are attempting to deploy symbolism and narrative to re-purpose abandoned urban infrastructure into urban public spaces. I have derived several research questions:

1. How do Friends of the Park organizations successfully navigate institutional settings to create public spaces?
2. How do Friends of the Park organizations involved in creating public spaces gain community, private, and governmental support?
3. How do Friends of the Park organizations involved in creating public spaces manage the discourse around these proposed spaces?

To analytically test these questions I use a mixed qualitative approach, combining in-depth interviews, document analysis, site visits, and census tract data. I focus on a selected contemporary phenomenon where in-depth descriptions would be an essential component of the process. In such situations, small qualitative studies can gain a more personal understanding of the phenomenon and the results can contribute valuable knowledge to the community. If a certain kind of unsuccessful discourse theme (or successful one) exhibits itself in a large portion of the potential population, you're very likely to see it in this sample; if the discourse exhibits itself in a very small portion, you're very unlikely to see it. Small samples, in other words, are a wide-mesh net, convenient for catching the big themes.

Keywords

infrastructure, institutional entrepreneurship, livable cities

Contents

Acknowledgments

This work would not have been possible without the financial support of Brown University, and the Hazeltine Fellowship. I am grateful to all of those with whom I have had the pleasure to work during this and other related projects. I would especially like to thank Dr. Meghan Kallman and Dr. Leslie Campbell, for reading and giving critical feedback on this project as it took shape. Nobody has been more important to me in the pursuit of this project than the members of my family—my parents, my loving and supportive husband, and our kids, who provide unending inspiration.

Introduction

Across the country, adding or expanding urban green space has been shown to both increase foot traffic and bring economic growth to a city. Communities across the United States and elsewhere have noticed the environmental, political, and economic advantages of urban green spaces; both advocacy and popularity have grown quickly in the last 20 years. A number of these green spaces are structured around current infrastructure or abandoned transportation infrastructure; both are credited with re-greening an area.

In 2015, Pittsburgh-based nonprofit Riverlife worked with consultants to estimate the economic benefits related to parks and trails, in their attempts to make an economic case for Pittsburgh's Three Rivers Park. The consultants reviewed four projects involving repurposing or adding urban green spaces—in Boston, Chattanooga, Atlanta, and Cincinnati. They found that in all four cases, return on the public investment (ROI) of adding green space ranged from at least 6:1 (Atlanta), to as high as 40:1 (Boston) (Riverlife, 2015). Over and above their use, city parks provide multiple kinds of economic benefits; boosting property values, increasing tourism, direct use, improving health, adding to community cohesion, and enhancing clean water and air.

Because of the different ways people experience parks, cities need to provide many kinds of parks, from neighborhood facilities to large natural areas. Many health benefits associated with parks can be achieved through small-scale, readily accessible sites. This includes providing contact with nature, increasing opportunities for physical activity, and mitigating climate, air, and water pollution impacts on public health (Harnik & Welle, 2009).

Urban park space is expensive to develop, and it can be challenging to create a park in a fully developed and built-out city. Efforts to add smaller green spaces have included developing public plazas, civic squares, greenways, gardens, pocket parks, and linear parks (pps.org). Because of the limited availability of open space near urban areas, and increasing land prices, government agencies, and advocacy groups began to consider and evaluate land not traditionally associated with parks.

Many types of manmade corridors, such as street rights-of-way and abandoned railroads (Bentryn, 1976) have been recycled for park or bicycle trail development. Abandoned industrial spaces, including train and bus stations and rail fragments, are usually close to former (and current) warehousing districts. These kinds of parks tend to come into contact with more private land than do traditional parks, and require complex coalition-building efforts throughout the development process.

In the United States, four Friends of the Park advocacy groups have attempted to turn abandoned industrial infrastructure into urban parks—two in New York City, and one each in Chicago and Philadelphia. Three of the advocacy groups have been active since 1999/2000, with a fourth coming later. Their successes and partial successes are the focus of this book.

In New York, Chicago, and Philadelphia—older, dense cities that can feel packed with people and are typically underserved by parks—trees and greenery are a blessing and a design opportunity. Opportunities to reuse old infrastructure, buildings, and spaces can change the way people interact with and think about their own neighborhoods—what deCerteau (1984) calls "the practice of the city" (1984:102). The parks profiled here are examples of how abandoned industrial spaces might be repurposed into something new.

All of these projects involve a change in perspective—either way above or way below city streets. New York's High Line, Chicago's Bloomingdale Trail/606, and parts of Philadelphia's Rail Park are elevated over streets at heights of 15 to 30 feet. Users are able to experience urban space in ways that are different from other public works, and achieve views of the urban landscape that would never otherwise be accessible. In the case of New York's High Line, the park provides a unique view of both the East and Hudson Rivers at the same time, among other design features. With the 606, the park takes users through four very different neighborhoods without ever having to cross a street.

In the case of Philadelphia's Rail Park, the potential park is both elevated and submerged in spots. The elevated part cuts at an angle across the grid of downtown Philadelphia, providing views not possible from street level. New York's Low Line, like part of the proposed Rail Park, is below ground, and plans to use cutting-edge technology to bring natural sunlight into a subterranean space. The 606 and the High Line are used as both public spaces and gathering spots for urban residents; the High Line is also New York City's top tourist destination.

Creating one of these parks requires an extended partnership among: city Parks departments, Public Works and/or Transportation departments, federal and state agencies, private sector citizen groups, foundations, and/or corporations. The political and structural issues are too extreme for government to handle without support from local citizenry; financial and legal issues are too complicated for the private sector to manage without public agency assistance. For many of these projects, much of the funding comes from some combination of federal, state, and local governments.

Projects like this generally need strong support from "Friends of" advocacy groups to make them happen. Advocates for the park must make the park's development story appeal successfully to different stakeholders, since successful parks draw upon multiple complementary constituencies to ensure strong levels of use (Jacobs, 1961). Some stakeholders are focused on the livability benefit, others are focused on economic returns.

Struggles over these parks can be viewed through multiple lenses, like the role of architecture and construction, the influence of money and politics on how spaces are used, and the roles played by culture, communication, and presentation in creating a community of interest in support of building these parks. Repurposing these spaces also takes a long time, usually well over 10 years, and is very expensive, costing tens of millions of dollars. So the groups need to raise a great deal of money, from public and private sources, over long periods of time, to be successful. The case studies incorporate the roles played by architects and designers, wealthy donors, community members, and governmental decision-makers in making something old new again. The role of the neighborhood is also considered, since what is old is physically anchored somewhere specific.

The role of economic interest in urban development has been well studied and well documented, but alone does not explain why individuals without a clear economic interest devote time and effort to making these parks a reality. Local entrepreneurs advocating for their projects need to tell a compelling story, to many different entities, over a long period of time, to build coalitions in support of proposed new public amenities. To date, the role of message in building coalitions in support of public space has not been well studied (Battilana and Dorado, 2010).

In the rest of this book, I evaluate attempts by four advocacy groups to frame and communicate the stories around these parks as part of their overall goal of building the parks. We know language has power, reflecting and contributing to social meanings and patterns. The words we use can affect how people make decisions about the distribution of urban rights and resources.

- Who gets to decide what kind of urban amenity gets built, and who it should be for?
- Who gets to decide how much is too much money to spend on an urban amenity?
- Since all of these projects rely on public money, should cities spend money to develop amenities primarily for their residents?
- Should cities spend money to develop amenities primarily for tourists, who then spend money elsewhere in the city?
- Should cities spend money to develop amenities that look nice, but are not multifunctional?
- Should cities decide to develop an amenity, if it benefits some groups—wealthier, more educated—while hurting the poor, people of color, older folks, and so on?

In order to understand the relevance of the communication themes these entrepreneurs present, each park needs to be seen in context. Important themes in some cases reflect the demographics of the cities, the long process of development, the ability to organize the community in support of the Park (or not), the influence of elites on the process (real and/or perceived), the challenges of building in these spaces, the ability of the Friends of the Park groups to create a shared common identity around development of these spaces, and so on.

Chapter 1 presents a short theoretical background and the methods used in these case studies. Chapter 2 presents a case study of New York's High Line and the efforts of the Friends of the High Line. Chapter 3 presents a case study of Chicago's Bloomingdale Trail/606 and the efforts of the Friends of the 606. Chapter 4 presents a case study of Philadelphia's Rail Park and the efforts of the Friends of the Rail Park. Chapter 5 presents a case study of New York's Low Line. Each of the case study chapters provides insight into how Friends of the Park groups do (or do not) form coalitions of support to turn abandoned infrastructure into parks. Chapter 6 provides a comparative chapter evaluating the common themes that cut across all cases, along with concluding thoughts.

New York's successful High Line may in fact not only be a new urban ethos that is manifestly public (definitely not privatized, not sequestered behind a wall) but also clearly a project of local real-estate capital. The in-process Low Line bears the (chosen) burden of a name similar to the High Line, in the same city, proposing a space perceived as elite. In contrast, the Philadelphia and Chicago parks (in-process and opened) are far less "elite" in public perception. Perceptions of these parks intersect with key discourse themes in both predictable and unexpected ways, and influence park development trajectories in all four cases.

CHAPTER 1

Theoretical Background and Methods

In New York (High Line and Lowline), Chicago (Bloomingdale Trail/606), and Philadelphia (Rail Park) between 1999 and 2017, nonprofit community groups have attempted to or have successfully created public–private coalitions to repurpose neglected urban public spaces into urban parks. These case studies are located in similar cities, the projects started around the same time (or were strongly influenced by each other), the groups are trying to do similar things, and yet the projects are in very different stages of project development.

These urban park projects combine long-term entrepreneurial efforts of advocacy groups with key site characteristics. Both have to be compelling and plausible in getting governments, philanthropists, wealthy individuals, and community members to take the project and the group seriously. The groups are actively trying to build coalitions of support, over long periods of time, and so need to demonstrate how capable and innovative they are. Each group has characteristics that can make it easier or harder to achieve its task, including how organized the group is, the kinds of skills the group has in organizing the community, whether the group is able to raise money, and whether there is any organized opposition.

The advocacy groups in each case are also actively trying to frame these abandoned spaces as something other than what they currently are. The reframing is tricky, because these objects are large, immovable, and unchanging, for at least 8 to 10 years. There are also site-specific attributes that could make the abandoned space more or less possible to be repurposed, including what neighborhoods it runs through, what condition it is in and how much it costs to make it a park, how users could actually access it, whether the city even needs a park in that location, and so on.

I use literature from the field of institutional entrepreneurship to explore how these entrepreneurs develop, communicate, and influence themes around their projects to build coalitions of support. Within the field of institutional entrepreneurship, I focus on the communication and presentation of conversation and media themes relying on links to existing organizational and institutional logics—how entrepreneurs show people the new thing they propose is real and makes sense, given how things *are supposed to* work. In using this literature, I am trying to understand how the entrepreneurs use strategic communication themes, whether the themes help or hurt them in making their case, and what kinds of themes make sense for the physical object they are attempting to repurpose (Plavin-Masterman 2013).

Institutional Logics: A Concise Review

Organizations live in an environment full of institutions (the state, the church, and so on). They have connections—personal, business, or both—to a variety of other organizations and institutions (Hoang and Antoncic 2003; Perry-Smith and Mannucci 2015). Being connected affects actions taken by the organizations' leaders (Friedland and Alford 1991). In effect, each of society's institutions—the market, the state, families, among others—have a central logic that provides context and constraints on individual and organizational behavior (Thornton and Ocasio 2008). The institutional logics also refer to a set of belief systems and associated practices (Reay and Hinings 2009), which affect how organizations are structured, how they carry out their work (Scott 2004), and *what we think institutions are supposed to look like and do*. To understand individual and organizational behavior, it must be seen in its institutional context.

The four advocacy groups studied here must attempt to reconcile competing logics of park development and economic growth as they attempt to repurpose an abandoned industrial space into a park. Those competing logics inflict different pressures on the advocacy groups in terms of what to discuss, who to target with messages, and how to attempt to influence project development. Based on Battilana, Leca, and Boxenbaum's 2009 review article, I define institutional entrepreneurs as *actors who leverage resources to create new or transform existing institutions* (DiMaggio 1988; Garud, Hardy, and Maguire 2007; Maguire and Hardy 2006) and apply this definition to the four advocacy groups studied. In all cases, the advocacy groups are trying to be seen as the organization with the right to speak for the space in question, and the group that can determine what happens to the space. The groups are trying to transform something that was not a park into a park, and do so in a way that has not been done before.

Like all entrepreneurs, these groups face pressures, often competing ones. Meeting those pressures is more challenging than for traditional entrepreneurs, as these institutional entrepreneurs combine nonprofit and for-profit institutional logics that have little in common. Reconciling these institutional logics into a coherent narrative is made more difficult when the process is one of redefinition or recreation (Lawrence and Suddaby 2006), making something new out of the shell of something existing, as in the case of the industrial spaces. In addition, these entrepreneurs face the challenge of solving a complex problem in an urban setting; no single organization, public or private, could undertake such a project on its own and hope to solve it. Thus, they need to rely on multiple public and private entities, and as a result, they have to balance multiple competing logics.

The extent to which these entrepreneurs resolve competing logics affects their venture's viability and sustainability (Battilana and Dorado 2010; Tracey, Phillips, and Jarvis 2011). Interest in competing logics has extended to investigating differing organizational mechanisms designed to manage these competing logics (Pache and Santos 2010; Reay and Hinings 2009), along with how entrepreneurs successfully broker among different logics (Bjerregard and Lauring 2012). Conflicting pressures stemming from brokering among different institutional logics can create ambiguity for organizational leaders and participants (Greenwood et al. 2011). Tracey, Phillips, and Jarvis (2011) highlight the challenges for these institutional entrepreneurs faced with having to reconcile competing institutional logics, using three related dimensions, envisioning, creating, and legitimating.

Envisioning discourse attempts to frame the entrepreneur's potential project as a solution to a gap in existing institutional arrangements. In the *envisioning* dimension of discourse, the work required to transform existing institutions or build new institutions focuses on the meaning behind actions (Scott 1994, 1995). Carrying out that work depends on communities of practice being willing to do the work to make the intended new institutions real (Lawrence and Suddaby 2006).

Creating discourse focuses on defining and establishing the organizational processes the entrepreneurs need to bring their desired project into existence. The entrepreneurs must show an organizational template, or otherwise highlight their capacity to make the venture happen. Discourse in this dimension usually involves some form of a roadmap and timeline that individuals see and hear about. And, *legitimating* discourse requires entrepreneurs to link their efforts to both higher-status, known actors and larger, macro-level conversations. For example, efforts to give a neighborhood meaning through strategic themes can strengthen the effect community organizations have on what the neighborhood can look like (Martin 2003a; Elwood 2006). Specifically, "state institutions, the private sector, and nongovernmental organizations all engage in a range of ... [behaviors]... through which they attempt to influence urban change and decision-making processes" (Elwood 2006, p. 324).

The 501c(3) groups studied here are making something for not just personal use, but also for the benefit of the larger community. The combination is in line with how Vargo and Lusch define service—resources for another party's benefit (Vargo and Lusch 2008, p. 26). Vargo and Lusch's concept of service-dominant logic (2004) provides a way to place the customer front and center into the conversation, asking, among other key questions, what is the service the 501c(3) is offering? How is that service embedded into physical objects, like the industrial infrastructure being repurposed? Tracy and Lyons (2013) explore service science concepts to include perception of value and resource exchange, specifically focusing on organizations that are not just profit-driven, like the 501c(3) groups.

The idea of aligning what service is being offered with what the customer is using it for fits with Tracey, Nelson, and Phillips' (2011) work on bridging or reconciling competing institutional logics. Vargo and Lusch's Axiom 5 (2016, p. 18) argues that value co-creation is coordinated through actor-generated institutions and institutional arrangements. Because of the nature of these projects, multiple actors interact in networks; the actions these actors take, in support of these new spaces, contribute to each other's wellbeing (Vargo and Lusch 2004, p. 10) by assisting in the development of these new urban public spaces. To bring these two streams together, value creation can occur in these settings when the 501c(3) groups successfully broker among competing institutional logics of park creation and urban development, and navigate the institutions and institutional arrangements that enable and constrain value creation (Vargo and Lusch 2016, p. 18).

Who the park is for is important when we consider the kind of communication themes used to encourage its development. There are those who live in the neighborhood and can benefit because they live near the proposed park. There are other beneficiaries who can be identified and appealed to, depending on the kinds of themes developed and presented—those who support the development of urban green space, for example, those who welcome the growth that comes with urban development, or even tourists. The parks can be considered common-pool resources (Ostrom 2008) and have many of the same kinds of problems of reconciling different interests and property rights spatially.

In New York, Chicago, and Philadelphia, gentrification[1] has occurred, is underway, or is hoped or projected for the areas around the park. Tensions created by gentrification processes add to the complexity of emotion around the places where people live. (Logan and Molotch 1987). This is especially true in the last 10 to 15 years, as the state has played more of an active role in gentrification, as federal disbursements have decreased (Hackworth and Smith 2001).

In addition, developers are pursuing gentrification projects in areas that need public support to mitigate their risk; their proposed projects could be in areas without enough local wealth or population to enable them to make money without a development subsidy. Inner-city investment economics have changed in ways that accelerate certain types of neighborhood change, including increased wealth and development—particularly in New York (Hackworth 2002).

---

[1] The process by which the middle-class (and the rich as well) begin to live in a traditionally working-class area of a city, changing the character of the area.

Contributions

City governments and urban planners know that green spaces and public spaces matter to urban dwellers. They also know that it is difficult to find large spaces to transform into green or public spaces; being creative in repurposing abandoned structures or sites is important (Plavin-Masterman 2013). The envisioning, creating, and legitimating (ECL) framework discusses the kind of activities required by the community groups interested in repurposing sites. First, these entrepreneurs have to explain why their proposed venture solves an existing problem—what the ECL framework calls *envisioning*. Next, entrepreneurs have to highlight their capacity to make the venture happen—what the ECL framework calls *creating*. Third, entrepreneurs have to link their efforts to both higher-status entities and larger, macro-level conversations—what the ECL framework describes as *legitimating*. As you might expect, the audiences for these kinds of work may not be the same, thus requiring the skills to make different, yet coherent arguments, to multiple groups.

Evaluating the communication around a given project is a useful way to structure the comparative study of these four *Friends of the Park* groups. There is a complicated balancing act performed by institutional entrepreneurs to reconcile competing themes (or not). Balancing efforts depend in part on the entrepreneur's ability to resolve conflicts between the institutional logics the entrepreneurs draw upon. The efforts also depend in part on the entrepreneurs' ability to use the park, as an object, to "invoke without explicitly arguing; this action can enhance or soothe the competition between different institutional logics" (Meyer et al. 2013, p. 527). And, resolving conflicts is critical for the success of these organizations; a common organizational identity "that strikes a balance between the logics the organization combines" enables sustainability (Battilana and Dorado 2010:1435).

In addition, not enough attention is paid to understanding where new firms come from, how they are organized, and how they evolve (Aldrich 1999). Many case studies of entrepreneurship focus on success stories. It is also important to compare successes and partial successes to shed more light on the process of entrepreneurship. The sites studied, evaluated over the same 16-year period, range from the completed (New York High Line,

Chicago) to the barely started (Philadelphia, New York Lowline). In addition, this book explores coalitions of community activists, politicians, and business elites joining in unexpected ways to develop public spaces.

Methods

New York, Chicago, and Philadelphia all have active park projects. The three cities are somewhat similar. New York, Chicago, and Philadelphia were ranked in the top 10 of cities around the country, based on the size of their population. New York ranked first with 8,391,881 people. Chicago ranked third with 2,851,268 people, and Philadelphia ranked sixth with 1,547,297 people (www.census.gov). These are densely settled cities, with a high ratio of developed areas per capita (such as high-rise buildings and commercial and industrial centers). As a result, residents of these kinds of cities need access to public parks.

The cities are all politically liberal, tending to vote for Democratic Party candidates. Both Philadelphia and New York are early colonial cities, and this history is reflected in their architecture and to some degree in their infrastructure, whereas Chicago is a city that came to prominence over a century later than either New York or Philadelphia.[2] Finally, the park locations are in each city's downtown areas, and share various similarities as shown in Table 1.1.

---

[2] New York developed a special relationship with Chicago that never existed between it and other United States cities: its *coronation* of Chicago as the western terminus of the Hudson River-Erie Canal-Great Lakes trade route to the nation's interior. New York pushed for Chicago's success to assure its own over east coast rivals like Boston and Philadelphia without the much sought for water route to the west. As a result, Chicago has always had a strong east coast connection. And, due to (1) the city's rise, (2) its power and energy during the industrialization and immigration that followed the Civil War, and (3) the development of American cities as social laboratories, Chicago's development during the era far more followed the route of Boston, New York, and Philadelphia than did its midwestern peers. This was especially true in terms of the city's population density, ethnic diversity, traffic, public transit, and so on (www.skyscrapercity.com, www.academicamerican.com).

Table 1.1 Summary of cases

Location	New York City – High Line	Chicago	Philadelphia	New York City – Lowline
Public space project	High Line	Bloomingdale Trail/606	Rail Park	The Lowline
Population living downtown rank (based on 2010 census)	1	2	3	1
Public space location within city	Chelsea, Meatpacking District	Humboldt Park/ Logan Square	Callowhill, Chinatown, Spring Garden, West Poplar	Lower East Side
Project status	Section 1 opened in 2009 Section 2 opened in 2011 Section 3 opened in 2014	In design process, Phase 1 opened in 2015 Phase 2 in process	City in process of obtaining complete stewardship Phase 1 under construction— expected to open 2018	Tentatively planned to open in 2021
Park size	1.5 miles (length)	2.65 miles (length)	2–3 miles (length depends on if the Reading Company transfers site control of 0.75 miles)	0.55 acres
Prior use	Freight line	Freight line	Passenger line and freight line	Trolley terminal
Cost	$240 million total	$91 million (estimated total)	$10.3 million Phase 1 $50–60 million (estimated total)	$83 million (estimated)
Community advocacy group	Friends of the High Line	Friends of the 606	Friends of the Rail Park	Underground Development Foundation
Park administration	Friends of the High Line (via contract with Parks Department)	Chicago Park District and Trust for Public Land	Philadelphia Department of Parks and Recreation	Underground Development Foundation (planned, via contract with Parks Department)

Approach

The process by which each *Friends of the Park* (FoTP) group brings the park into existence is related in large part to the group's ability to influence the themes and descriptions that are used in discussing their plan for the space (Plavin-Masterman 2013). Can these groups shape the discussion while ensuring they appeal successfully to multiple stakeholders? *What is it* about specific themes that matter, and how does that change over time? Are the messages about the entrepreneur, the FoTP group, consistent? Are they complementary to or contradicted by messages about the proposed park, itself?

In order to answer these questions, I created case studies of the four projects, using multiple kinds of qualitative data, including mapping each site, interviewing key people, and examining media and documents for key themes. Mapping the sites physically included geocoding them, physically walking on and around the locations, and recording my observations as an observer—what are the sites like, where are they located, how do you get to them, what is around them, and so on. Figure 1.1 shows the High Line passing under the Standard Hotel.

Figure 1.1 High Line park, New York

Source: M. Plavin-Masterman

In Chicago, Figure 1.2 illustrates a sense of the Trail/606 seen in context in the neighborhood, as the Trail is 16 feet off the ground and yet is dwarfed by the "El" passing overhead.

Figure 1.2 606 with view down to playground

Source: Victor Grigas/Wikimedia Commons/Bloomingdale Trail, the 606, Chicago 2015-34.jpg

In Philadelphia, Figure 1.3 shows a view of Center City from the undeveloped Rail Park.

Figure 1.3 Center City, as seen from an elevated section of the undeveloped Rail Park

Source: M. Plavin-Masterman

The Lowline Lab was a simulated setup open to the public for approximately two years. The undeveloped space is not open to the public. Figure 1.4 shows an interior shot of the lab.

Figure 1.4 Lowline Lab, New York

Source: M. Plavin-Masterman

My document analysis evaluated which communication themes were and are important in each case and could influence organizations and the park's development trajectory. What kinds of themes did the Friends of the High Line, Friends of the Bloomingdale Trail/606, Friends of the Rail Park, and the Lowline engage in? With whom? Who engaged the community? How? Using what images, what words? In all cases, I looked for fragmentation in a theme, inconsistency among speakers, and variance over time. Using the ECL framework of Tracey, Phillips, and Jarvis (2011), I coded data into themes according to the different forms of institutional work that the entrepreneurs performed—envisioning, creating, and legitimating (2011, p. 64). In each of the cases, I evaluated themes, consistency or difference in how these themes were treated over time, and particular unusual patterns in the data. I then reviewed what, if any, sub-themes appeared consistently over time, or were unique or time-specific occurrences. Finally, I reviewed each theme to understand whether there were gaps in the discourse, and if so, for how long.

CHAPTER 2

Friends of the High Line: How Two Guys Became a Parks Conservancy

The High Line was built as a freight railroad line to serve Manhattan's West Side. It opened in 1934, and closed in 1980, sitting neglected and abandoned for decades. Chelsea neighborhood residents Robert Hammond and Joshua David met at a public forum in 1999 discussing whether or not to save the High Line, and decided to work together to preserve it, founding the Friends of the High Line (FHL) as the organizing entity. The story of the High Line's proposed demolition, preservation, and eventual redesign as a public park has caught the attention of artists, architects, city planners, celebrities, business entrepreneurs, and writers worldwide.

The FHL founders, Hammond and David, positioned themselves as the leading open space advocate group in their community—the sparsely populated Chelsea and Meatpacking neighborhoods. The FHL was also able to leverage social networks that included people with access to power, influence, and money (Behance Team 2009; Svendsen 2010; Benepe 2012). In 2005, New York City's Bloomberg administration assumed control of the former rail line, and in 2006, ground was broken. Section One of the High Line opened to the public in June 2009, Section Two opened in June 2011, and Section Three opened in 2014. Figure 2.1 shows the High Line relative to its neighborhoods.

Under an agreement with the New York City, FHL manages the maintenance and operations of the park (Hammond 2011; Benepe 2012). The High Line has turned into one of the most innovative and inviting public spaces in the New York City, attracting over seven million visitors in 2016; since 2012, it has been New York City's most popular tourist

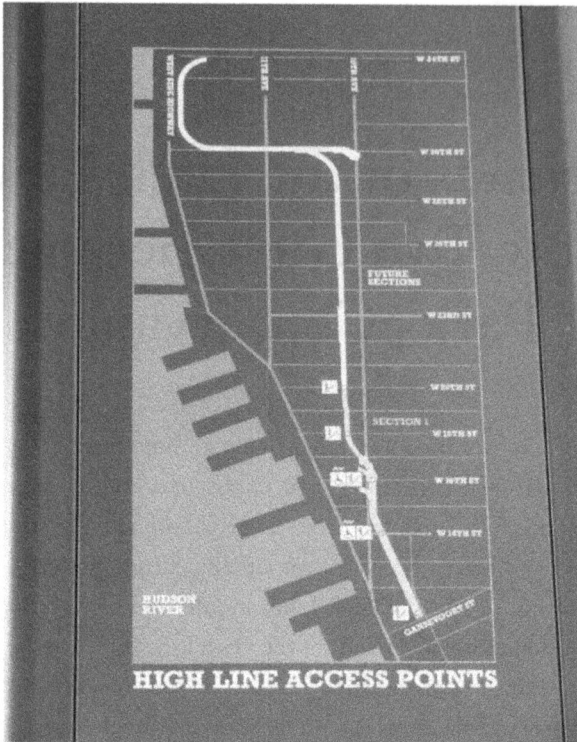

Figure 2.1 High Line park map

Source: By Reinhard Dietrich (own work) [CC0], via Wikimedia Commons.

destination (thehighline.org). When you first see the High Line, it looks exactly like the kind of thing urban parks were created to get away from; it is a heavy structure supporting an elevated rail line, that looks, (until you get close) more like an abandoned relic than an urban green oasis.

The FHL can be considered successful institutional entrepreneurs because they managed to develop and support several key themes around how the park would look, how they would actually get the park open, and how the park would fit in with the surrounding neighborhoods. In support of these themes, the FHL used public presentations wherever possible, to show current and future High Line images. They also strategically used interviews, fundraisers, and other gatherings where they could meet people to build connections and again show images. Over time, the themes around the park changed slightly, from "High Line as urban oasis" (Del Signore 2012) to High Line as both urban oasis *and* gentrification spark. This change is reflected in the different tones in the discourse around the park pre- and post-opening.

As with the Rail Park in Philadelphia (discussed in more detail in Chapter 4), the abandoned High Line was generally seen as an agent of blight, limiting economic development. Its structure cast dark shadows, areas under the tracks attracted unsavory and illegal activities, and business owners faced challenges in using land parcels efficiently for development or redevelopment (Hammond and David 2011). In fact, in the 1980s, soon after the last rail car left the High Line, adjacent property owners began clamoring to tear down the remaining tracks. Rudolph Giuliani, New York's mayor for much of the 1990s, could not wait to tear down the High Line (Behance Team 2009). His administration, aware that Chelsea was slowly gentrifying into a neighborhood of galleries, restaurants, and loft living, believed the High Line remnant was an ugly deadweight (Goldberger 2011). They were convinced this reminder of a different kind of city had to be removed for the neighborhood to realize its full potential. But, in fact, almost a decade after the Giuliani administration tried to tear the High Line down, it was turned into one of the most innovative and inviting public spaces in New York City.

A Brief History of Civic Action

In an interview with CNN in 2007, Joshua David and Robert Hammond, the co-founders of FHL described how they got started. David said that he lives down the street from the High Line in Chelsea in Manhattan, and for many years never paid attention to it, as it is nestled between buildings in Chelsea (Hammond and David 2007). Hammond added that he read in *The New York Times* that they were going to tear down the High Line, and learned that the sections of it were all connected—something observers could not tell from the street level. Hammond thought some group would be working to preserve it, so he went to a community meeting to volunteer. (David and Hammond 2007)

Hammond and David ended up at the same community meeting and realized no one else wanted to save the High Line. They befriended each other and began a campaign *out of their kitchens* (Hammond 2007;

Hammond and David 2011). Their initial goal was simply preserving the High Line. Many community-based organizations, especially those focused on urban planning, started trying to stop something from happening (Elwood 2006). There was a degree of that when Hammond and David started, as illustrated by the following quote.

> Mayor Giuliani at the time wanted to tear it down, so at first we were fighting just to keep it. But the goal long term was always to bring the public up here. It was such a magical experience for us; we wanted to make it public... It's an interesting feeling because you see the New York skyline in the background—the Empire State Building and the Chrysler Building—and you have this great juxtaposition with the wildflowers and the grasses (David and Hammond 2007).

Hammond and David may have met by chance, and had no professional experience in urban planning, politics, or real estate development; they did, however, have important skills for deploying a successful urban park campaign. Both had direct experience negotiating, organizing, and programming. Hammond was a consultant for several endeavors nonprofits, including the Times Square Alliance, Alliance for the Arts, and National Cooperative Bank (NCB), in addition to being an artist (thehighline.org). David was a freelance magazine writer and editor for Gourmet, Fortune, Travel + Leisure, Wallpaper, and others (thehighline. org). Both are very involved in the gay community based in Chelsea, and are said to have influential partners in the world of entertainment and media. Hammond describes the Chelsea gay community as providing many early supporters (Behance Team 2009).

In addition, the neighborhood was not particularly residential, and there were relatively few organized neighborhood groups. The FHL did have to manage opposition, especially from property owners with air development rights under the existing High Line structure. The opposition is not all that surprising given the urban planning implications of doing something with the real estate occupied by the High Line. At the time the FHL got started, the discourse around the High Line itself represented the structure as unhealthy and decaying. Tearing it down was framed as providing opportunities for capital investment.

The two cofounders launched an appeal linking saving the High Line to improved public life. Their pleas to save the High Line captivated many influential New Yorkers (Hammond 2011; Benepe 2012). Famed designer Diane von Furstenberg, a long-time Meatpacking District resident, contributed her time, contacts, studio, and money (von Furstenberg 2011). Former Parks Commissioner Benepe pointed out that the city began to support this initially *wacky idea* (Benepe 2012) when they realized that the FHL were forming a conservancy to operate the High Line, and that FHL was able to raise funds from wealthy philanthropists and celebrities for the High Line's development.

The first step in the process of converting the High Line into a park was to legally prevent its demolition. In order for the federal government to approve tearing down the line under Federal Surface Transportation Board guidelines, requesting parties were required to provide evidence that adequate resources existed for demolition. Before the FHL got involved, no one had asked the city to confirm this money was actually available. The FHL did outreach immediately, to raise money to sue New York City's government in 2001 and force the city to provide this information (Hammond 2009).

According to city planners, the election in 2001 of Michael Bloomberg as the mayor was a critical turning point (Svendsen 2010; Burden 2011; Stone 2012; Benepe 2012). The project itself appealed to Mayor Bloomberg's agenda, which included support for the arts, public education, business, and improving the quality of the local environment (Greco 2011; Benepe 2012). Andrew Stone, New York City Director, Trust for Public Land agreed with the key role played by the mayor's office in the High Line's development:

> Bloomberg's getting elected mayor was a huge advance for the Friends of the High Line. They had political struggles and technical struggles. Technical struggles including everything from engineering feasibility to fundraising, and political struggles being it's extremely hard to move something like this without the support of the mayor. So clearly, if you kind of say that those are the two big struggles and like half of it is the political, like well, that the election of the mayor changed things so much (Stone 2012).

In many ways, the High Line became a favorite issue of politicians; they heard from constituencies not normally involved in community development (Behance Team 2009). While developers, decision makers, politicians, and the public considered potential designs, the FHL pressed ahead with legal action to stop the demolition while raising money for reconstruction. Despite efforts to build public support and financing, early opposition to the High Line by the development community was intense and the rail line came close to destruction.

In the final analysis over whether to go forward with the High Line's redevelopment, it came down to a cost–benefit analysis. Mayor Bloomberg asked his then-Deputy Mayor for Economic Development, Daniel Doctoroff, to decide whether or not the High Line was economically viable over the long term. An advisor of the FHL described an exchange between FHL and the Mayor's Office:

Doctoroff came to us and said,

> Hey, I don't care about all these pretty pictures,—we have so many parks and we can barely maintain them as it is. So, we did an economic feasibility study. …We said if we could prove that in over 20 years the incremental tax revenues to the city will be greater than the project cost—even though the city is not going to pay for it and we find that it is actually buildable and you can actually do it, would you get on board? And he said, 'Yes' (Fuchs 2011).

In 2005, New York City joined New York State, CSX Transportation and Conrail (the current and former owners of the High Line) in applying for federal approval to convert the structure to permanent public space through the federal rail-banking program. In November 2005, Mayor Bloomberg announced that New York City had acquired the High Line from CSX Transportation; the city and CSX signed a trail-use agreement that allowed the 1.45-mile rail remnant to be used for public recreation. The title transfer and the trail-use agreement, concluded on November 4, 2005, were the final legal steps necessary to transform the High Line (Amateau 2005).

While the city pursued acquisition, and with the Grand Central Station and Times Square redevelopments as precedents, New York's City

Planners rezoned the area around the High Line and changed it into an arts district to attract tourists and art-related businesses.[1] The City Council approved the Special West Chelsea District in 2005, and this created a High Line Transfer Corridor, approximately 100 feet wide and including the High Line and adjacent lots between West 18th and West 30th Streets. Owners of property under the High Line could transfer air development rights[2] to other designated sites within the special district, preserving views around the High Line without compromising the park's light and air (Department of City Planning 2005; Svendsen 2010; Benepe 2012 Interview).

FHL Board Chair Phil Aarons actively supported this approach, arguing, "if the High Line was going to be saved, the development rights over the High Line were going to have to land somewhere. And wherever they landed, you would have taller buildings" (Hammond and David 2011, p. 23). Rezoning worked; developers were ultimately happier than they would have been if the High Line had been torn down (Hammond 2011 Interview).

Section One of the High Line opened to great acclaim and crowds in June 2009 at a cost of 85 million U.S. dollars, including public and private funding. Section Two of the High Line also opened to acclaim at a cost of 64 million U.S. dollars in June 2011; soon huge crowds began converging on it. In November 2011, FHL announced successful negotiations to secure the last piece of the High Line, the northern portion of the line that runs from 30th to 34th Streets, within the West Side Rail

---

[1] In the late 1990s, the Department of City Planning created a zoning mechanism for a new theater sub-district that allowed the transfer of development rights from certain theaters to other sites in the sub-district. This enabled both property and business owners in Times Square to renovate vacant buildings and improve streetscapes (Svendsen 2010).

[2] Property owners under the High Line had air "development rights," or the right to build up if the High Line were demolished. Preserving the High Line meant that those owners could not build up, and would lose out on the ability to turn development rights into economic benefit. Transferring their rights to other owners, who could then build higher, meant that all owners affected by the High Line would either be compensated or allowed to build.

Yards (Hammond 2011). Section Three, also known as *High Line at the Rail Yards*, opened in 2014, at a cost of 35 million U.S. dollars.

Under an agreement with the city, FHL manages the maintenance and operations of the park, with responsibility for an annual maintenance and operations budget of approximately five million dollars (Hammond 2011; Benepe 2012). Of that, at least two million dollars are dedicated solely to maintenance and operations and the remaining money is used for programming targeted toward children and the local community (David and Hammond 2011; Hammond 2011).

Discourse Themes as Mechanism for Reconciling Competing Logics

Before Section One opened, the themes of aesthetic or design, neighborhood, and FHL or coalition accounted for 67 percent of the total coded discourse. Interestingly, even though aesthetics or design is a strong theme, the pre-opening discourse is heavily weighted toward the creating and legitimating dimensions of institutional work these entrepreneurs have performed in order to make their project a reality, as opposed to envisioning discourse. The discourse is consistent in tone and mostly neutral or positive. The only exceptions are the development or cost theme and gentrification subtheme within the neighborhood theme, which are neutral or negative in tone.

From pre- to post-opening, the discourse around the High Line shifted in several ways. First, there was an increased focus on aesthetics, or the look of the park. Second, there was an increased focus on the cost of the project, as parts of the project opened and more construction was planned for other sections. The emphasis on FHL's capacity to create the park somewhat diminished in importance, as the first section served as a proof of concept. The original emphasis on the neighborhood decreased dramatically and the discourse began to split in the neighborhood theme. While issues were raised as far back as 2006, it is not until the High Line opened that the opposing side gained traction in the discourse and affected the overall tone.

Percentage of discourse dedicated to type of institutional work, high line park,
New York, 2000–2016

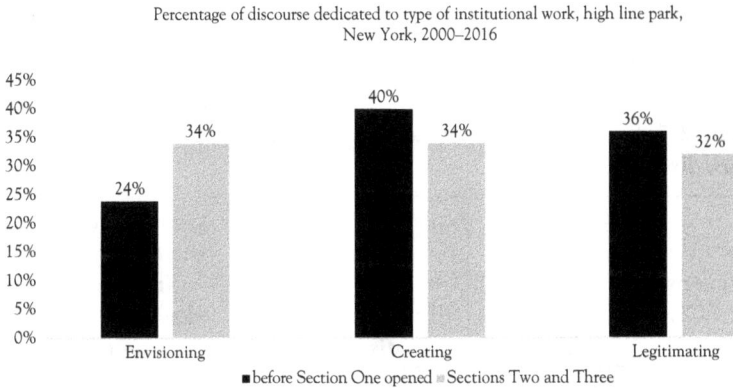

Figure 2.2 Shows a comparison of pre- and post-opening dimensions of the discourse

The post-opening discourse also reflected a nearly even split among the three dimensions, in contrast to pre-opening discourse that focused on creating and legitimating institutional dimensions, as seen in Figure 2.2. Aesthetics and design also became much more important in the post-opening discourse. The post-opening balance reflects less urgency in the creating dimension, since the project opened. The balance may also reflect less urgency to focus on the neighborhood theme in the legitimating dimension, because the project can only be where it is, which is in the Chelsea or Meatpacking neighborhood. The post-opening balance, however, glosses over the discord in certain parts of the discourse, particularly in the case of the neighborhood theme—a trend that intensified after 2011, with the opening of the second part of the High Line.

While most of the discourse is still positive in tone, there has been an increase in the amount of negative discourse since the High Line opened. Post-opening, the discourse generally appears more balanced among the three dimensions of institutional work than the pre-opening discourse did. However, nearly 20 percent of the discourse since 2009 is negative in tone, as compared to approximately 10 percent of the discourse pre-opening. The largest proportion of the negative discourse is located in the legitimating dimension—not surprising given the tensions between the

FHL and the neighborhood. Table 2.1 summarizes how themes appear in the discourse over time.

Table 2.1 Summary of themes within dimensions in the High Line Park discourse

Dimension of ECL work	Theme	Tone of theme in discourse	Consistent use of theme in articles, interviews, discussions, and presentations
Envisioning	Aesthetic or design	Pre- and post-opening: positive or neutral	Pre- and post-opening: Yes
Envisioning	Access or usability	Pre- and post-opening: positive or neutral	Pre- and post-opening: Yes
Envisioning	Art and artists	Pre- and post-opening: positive	Pre- and post-opening: Yes
Envisioning	History	Pre-opening: positive or neutral	Pre- and post-opening: Yes
Creating	FHL or coalition	Pre- and post-opening: positive or neutral	Pre- and post-opening: Yes
Creating	Development or cost	Pre-and post- opening: neutral or slightly negative in discussion of cost versus investment	Pre-and post-opening: Mostly
Legitimating	City	Pre-and post-opening: positive	Pre- and post-opening: Yes
Legitimating	Green	Pre-and post-opening: neutral	Pre-and post-opening: Yes
Legitimating	Neighborhood	Pre-and post-opening: subtheme changes or gentrification—neutral or negative Pre-and post-opening: subtheme of neighborhood revitalization— neutral or positive	Pre-opening consistent within each subtheme, but split overall Post-opening: negative tone of gentrification subtheme strongly consistent and dominates the more fragmented revitalization theme
Legitimating	Similar or other projects	Pre-and post-opening: positive or neutral	Pre-and post-opening: Yes

Envisioning: Aesthetics or Design

Envisioning work involves reframing the High Line to show how it solves a problem that prior institutional arrangements could not. The dominant theme in this category was aesthetics or design, and most of the discourse around that theme is positive. Some negativity appears early on in the project's development, which can be attributed to the blight of the existing structure and how project opponents were characterizing the High Line. Later, there is some discontent with some of the design choices made by High Line designers in response to private donors.

As de Moncheaux (2017) highlights, the High Line, benefitted from generous private funding and

> it's worth wondering what else seeps into public space—not the least of which seems to be a taste for order....Because you can't get too cute on a narrow platform 30 feet up, it requires more rules than some parks—but perhaps not as many as it has. Although its look evokes the thrillingly unplanned combination of infrastructure and wilderness that inspired the preservation of the overgrown viaduct, its defining detail is the prim arrangement of metal pins and ropes that enforce the border between paving and planting. They seem to say: Do not wander, do not play, do not fool around. (de Moncheaux 2017)

The High Line's style incorporated the neighborhood's grittiness and the structure's former states of decay and neglect. Hammond and David were nostalgic and romantic about having a train running through the neighborhood (James Corner Field Operations et al. 2015). Part of what makes the connection to the past so much part of the aesthetic is the idea of the park as elevated promenade (Mogul 2005), creating and enabling movement across public and private boundaries. But, Hammond and David also recognized that the High Line was loud, crowded, and dirty for those who actually had lived next to the train while it was in service. It was this sense of grittiness (Hotz 2005), of abandonment, (Perez 2004; Mogul 2005), link to a bygone era (Amateau 2006; Smith 2006), and a sense of illicitness (David and Hammond 2011) that contributed to the park's design.

Figure 2.3 Undeveloped High Line, pre-2000

Source: Reprinted from NYC.gov West Chelsea Zoning Proposal, 2005.

Adam Gopnik wrote a New Yorker article in 2001, accompanied by striking photographs like the one shown in Figure 2.3; people had started talking about the High Line. FHL and its supporters built on this set of images and consistently used words like *dreamy* (Hotz 2005), *one of a kind* (Amateau 2006), *magical* (David and Hammond 2007), *unusual* (Smith 2006), *stroller's paradise* (Schmerler and Simonson 2007), *urban wonderland* (Topousis 2007), and *secret* (Robinson 2005) to highlight how different the potential public space would be.

Hammond and David also consistently focused on the amount of space available without calling it a park, arguing that there were few chances for the city to design *1.5 miles of Manhattan* (McGraw Hill Construction 2003; Robinson 2005; David and Hammond 2011; Hammond 2011). This is similar to the work done by Friends of the Bloomingdale Trail/606 (FBT) in Chicago, where there is little emphasis on the green-ness of the project. This emphasis in New York is notable, given the lack of neighborhood green space in Chelsea and the Meatpacking District.

The High Line takes pedestrians through places they ordinarily cannot go. Being three stories up is just enough to alter the user's point of view. Hammond remembers that actually taking people up onto the High Line and then getting them to tell others about the experience was one of the most effective ways of selling early potential supporters on the site's aesthetic and design (Hammond 2011). FHL also showed High Line images whenever possible in their talks and presentations. FHL explicitly embraced the physical object as media and discourse strategy (Meyer et al. 2013).

In another example of the role of design in envisioning the project, as construction started, the work required new ballast, with sections of the old rail ties and rails replaced. "We don't want people to forget that the High Line was a railroad, [so t]he rail ties and rails will be numbered and stored so that we can replace them wherever appropriate" (David, via Amateau 2006). In addition, the team realized they could not keep the self-sown vegetation on the High Line; the weeds, grass, bushes, and trees had to be removed. As much as possible, plantings were designed to reproduce what was there and the new ballast was designed to accept new wind-sown seeds.

Discourse on the aesthetics of the space can drive home constraints and opportunities; both make the project feel more real. If stakeholders are debating where to put benches, or what they should look like, they have, implicitly, already bought in to the project happening. This tactic has been used by real estate agents and car dealers, among others. Real estate agents encourage potential buyers to think of a room as fulfilling a certain function—office, nursery—or being able to accommodate a particular piece of furniture, such as a grand piano or large flat-screen television. Car dealers encourage potential buyers to discuss car colors, accessories, and options before any pricing discussions. The tactic is designed to change the entire discussion to one focused on *getting it to look right*, as opposed to *should we do it?* The design in this case had implications for how the High Line would be viewed by those in the immediate neighborhood and beyond. As Andrew Stone of TPL's New York office pointed out:

Accommodating neighborhood people? It's sort of like, 'Not really.' It's like, the High Line is amazing. It's one of a kind, but it wasn't designed to have accommodating neighborhood residents as one of its guiding principles. The reality is, ... that the design of the High Line is for, for me, is a particular kind of regional resource first and foremost. It's almost like you make certain decisions in your master plan and your overall design, and I think that it's designed as a regional resource—and a very particular kind of regional resource that's appealing to tourists. It has a real wow factor. (Stone 2012)

Soon after the High Line opened, the park, the High Line's designers, and the FHL began to win awards for various aspects of the project: this theme of the award-winning project, or award-winning design began to recur throughout the discourse. In short order, the High Line won a spot on the New Yorker's list of *10 Most Positive Architectural Events of 2009*, the International Association of Art Critics (IACA) First Prize for *Best Show in a Public Space* (2009), and the New York Landmarks Conservancy's Lucy G. Moses Preservation Project Award (2010). The Department of City Planning's 2005 West Chelsea Rezoning[3] won the Urban Land Institute's 2009 Global Award for Excellence. The High Line's team of designers won the New York Chapter of the American Institute of Architects' (AIA) Design Award for Urban Design (2010), and the American Society of Landscape Architects' (ASLA) 2010 General Design award. That same year, the cofounders of FHL were awarded the Jane Jacobs medal for New Ideas and Activism (Lindquist 2010). Despite the FHL's connections to city planners and celebrities, the awards were arms-length, due to the James Corner Field Operations or DS+R (diller scofidio + renfro) design, and not to the FHL's social network.

The cofounders began making the rounds of the lecture circuits. There, they continued to talk about the project in terms of its vision, which was to bring the experience of being up on this *amazing structure and seeing the city from this very special vantage point* (David and Hammond 2010) to the New York City. This strategy involved pictures of the High Line before and after, wherever possible. They talked about

---

[3] Rezoning preserved the High Line, and created a High Line air and light corridor through setback requirements.

the first section itself in terms of its design features, including a water feature, a sundeck, the "snazzy pathways of smooth concrete planks and the backless, thin, peel-up benches" (Kilgannon 2010). Hammond also commented that:

People really love [the High Line's movable chairs]. It gives them a sense of control over the space. We looked at having the designers design the chairs. They came up with all these different kind of chairs, but in the end we just used regular Parisian park chairs that you see all over parks all over the world. They're light, they're a simple design, and it's fascinating to see how many people use them in different configurations (Hammond 2012).

And, FHL continued to sell the vision of Sections Two and Three, by describing the flyover, the lawn space, 4,200 square feet, that anywhere else would be considered almost inconsequential—that, in New York, would be *just right for picnics* (Amateau 2010), and a viewing spur with an empty frame where a billboard used to be. They focused on describing the second section as smaller and more intimate, somehow, than the first (Kilgannon 2010), playing up the voyeuristic elements. The second section runs right up next to windows of residential buildings. "It feels like a Venetian canal, compared to the southern part…Like you're walking through the set of 'Rear Window'" (Benepe, quoted in Kilgannon 2010). This part of their media strategy, again using the physical object itself, relied on a combination of pictures of the space and encouraging visitors to go to the High Line's open section.

The High Line became a shorthand for innovative urban projects, its design used as a standard against which other projects were measured (Waite 2011). Other urban projects, with varying levels of similarity, got *High Line* added to their names: Philadelphia's High Line (Saffron 2009), Chicago's High Line (Eakin 2012), Mexico City's High Line (Samuelson 2011), Vancouver's High Line (Pablo 2009), and so on. FHL and the High Line's design team took this as a real affront, and in the discourse, they attempt to differentiate the High Line's aesthetic, but not necessarily its function, from these other projects. In a talk given in 2011, after Section Two opened, the architectural firm DS+R stressed that calling these other projects *High Line* does not ensure they can capture the High Line's effect. DS+R's Renfro argued that,

Everybody thinks that they can put a Bilbao up, y'know, a copy. I don't see how these cities could think that just having an elevated train line makes for a success—the kind of success we've seen with the High Line. (Diller, Scofido, and Renfro 2011)

Robert Hammond expressed his opinion that

in Chicago and Philadelphia they use 'High Line' to describe the function of the park—it's elevated and was a rail line, but not the aesthetic, since that has to be driven by the local community needs. Not every community wants their park to look like the High Line. (Hammond 2011)

This argument is somewhat disingenuous. In terms of design renderings and showing what the proposed parks could be, other projects, especially Philadelphia's Rail Park and New York's Lowline, rely on the phrase High Line specifically to conjure up images of that park and use it to generate support for their own projects.

Creating: FHL and Coalition of Supporters

The creating category of institutional work uses discourse to highlight the capacities and skills of the FHL to carry out the project. The dominant theme in this category was the FHL, themselves (who made themselves highly visible) and their work on raising money and building supporters as they became a conservancy managing the High Line. This theme accounted for 19 percent of the pre-opening discourse, and most of the discourse around that theme is positive. The development or cost theme is addressed initially in positive or neutral ways, and negative messages about this theme do not appear until later in the discourse, after the project opened.

While working on community-building efforts, FHL began to assemble connections to and highlight government agency members and wealthy private individuals. They relied initially on connections; social ties play a key role in entrepreneurial activity (Sorenson and Audia 2000; Hoang and Antoncic 2003; Jack 2010). Social ties enabled the FHL to access a variety of resources—information, advice, problem-solving, and so on—held by others.

One key example of the strength of social ties is what happened once Gifford Miller, City Council member and former college roommate of Robert Hammond's, changed his mind about the High Line. In 1999, he told Hammond, "saving an old rail line was a stupid idea" (Hammond and David 2011); by 2002, he had become an ardent supporter. He and others in the City Council began passing resolutions in support of the High Line, and Miller began making introductions to other City Council members, who in turn made introductions to other members of government. As a City Council Speaker, Miller earmarked 15 million U.S. dollars to plan and design the park, and U.S. Representative Jerrold Nadler (D-N.Y.) included five million U.S. dollars for the High Line in the House version of the 2005 six-year federal transportation bill (Hotz 2005).

The public was made aware of how much progress FHL was making, and how they had convinced the government and private individuals to support the project in the media, via newspapers and images, as well as on the High Line itself. When Section One of the High Line opened, the FHL was very creative with sponsorship, allowing organizations and individuals to put their names on parts of the High Line, including the Diller-von Furstenberg Sundeck (thehighline.org) and collecting private donations for other specific features such as 10th Avenue Square (Topousis 2007)—what Charles Isherwood of The New York Times calls "The graffiti of the philanthropic class" (Isherwood 2007).

Section Two of the High Line opened in June 2011. Like Section One, Section Two contained named features like the Falcone Flyover[4] (thehighline.org). Section Two of the Park also received acclaim and crowds. Figure 2.4 shows an image from Section Two post-opening.

Of the millions of annual visitors, approximately 50 percent were tourists and 50 percent were from Greater New York—with half of the latter

---

[4] The Falcone Flyover contains an elevated walkway eight feet above the High Line that allows visitors to look down onto trees and plantings on a spur of the original freight line that has not been developed for walking.

Figure 2.4 High Line Park's center section at 29th Street, which opened in June 2011

Source: By Jim Henderson (own work) [CC0], via Wikimedia Commons.

group from the surrounding neighborhoods (Humm 2012; Benepe 2012). Section Three opened in 2014 to a different kind of acclaim.

> With more limited construction funds, the strategy in this part of the park was bare bones: Rusty tracks are filled in with bonded gravel to make a level path; timber dunnage is stacked to make a bleacher from which people can peer out at the water and over the rail yards..... giving visitors a glimpse of how the High Line looked before its makeover. (Zimmerman 2014)

Focusing on FHL's abilities to raise money and get government support reassures community members, government agencies, and potential donors that the group can actually make the project happen. The FHL focused on raising money for construction, not maintenance, and their choice not to create an endowment or some sort of neighborhood improvement district for ongoing maintenance and operations was glossed over in the pre-opening discourse; it is not clear why. This focus in the discourse kicked the can down the road. As a result of choosing to focus on construction instead of maintenance and operations before opening Section One, the FHL has been forced to remain in fundraising mode to keep the park going. The development discourse around the park has been full of sour notes post-opening, due to FHL's response to this funding shortfall and what were seen as high project construction and operating costs.

First, there was an attempt to create a business improvement district, where the community would close the gap in the park's operating costs with a tax exclusively on those living near the High Line (Kovaleski 2009). That proposal made the adjacent businesses furious and failed. The FHL also tried to persuade the buildings abutting the High Line to pay annual fees. The Standard Hotel does embed a High Line fee in its room charges, but some of the other buildings balked.

While many surrounding building owners are happy to have the traffic and associated revenues related to millions of annual visitors, they do not want to pay extra for it. The residential building Caledonia, for example, was asked to pay 800,000 U.S. dollars annually for use of a door as an easement:

> The building always knew it would have to pay a fee to the Parks Department for this access point: the building built and provided a bathroom and elevator that the City has an easement to access. But asking for 800,000 U.S. dollars a year for the use of a door is excessive and out of touch with reality [so the door is never opened]. (Steinberg 2012)

Legitimating: Neighborhood

Before Section One opened, this part of the discourse focused on connecting the supporting rationales of the project to larger discussions about the Chelsea or Meatpacking neighborhood. The first subtheme, by far the most dominant, involves how the High Line both respects the neighborhood's history and provides a needed amenity to residents. The tone of this theme is primarily positive or neutral in the pre-opening section of the discourse. The second subtheme involves the effects the park will have on the current process of gentrification, its impact on lower-income residents, and those residents' perception that perhaps the High Line is not for them. This theme appears, in one way or another, in all cases.

Before opening Section One, the FHL and its supporters focused on the idea that the High Line would revitalize the neighborhood. FHL tried to engage the community actively, through school-based and other local programming. They linked development of the High Line to increased amenities for residents. The FHL did this through discussion of the Whitney Museum and the arts and gallery district, through talking up the benefits of increased density and pedestrian traffic in a relatively sparsely populated section of Manhattan, and through planning to have a significant amount of park programming be locally focused (Humm 2012; highline.org).

FHL also pushed hard to link the High Line's history to revitalizing the neighborhood. "It was built to move in eggs and butter to factories in New York City. Now it can be used to move people in and out of the galleries, restaurants, apartments and offices that those warehouses have become" (Hammond, via Burghart 2003). City officials argued that the High Line was a *critical element* in the city's west-side revitalization plan (Doctoroff, via Burghart 2003), and it would prop up that area (Benepe 2012).

As articles began appearing citing the positive responses of community leaders and business owners toward the new project, the FHL again focused on the community base of support. "The High Line is about a group of community members who rallied around it" (David, via Humm 2012); the FHL believe that it is those community roots that have made it so successful. Gallery owners praised the city's commitment to public space (Robinson 2005), saying the project would be good for everyone in the neighborhood. Other retailers were optimistic about increased pedestrians and activity. They especially highlighted the impact on the art galleries (Robinson 2005) and the Whitney Museum's future move to Gansevoort Street, at the High Line lower terminus (Day 2015).

Projected public taxes and private investment opportunities related to the High Line project proved to be an attractive idea to private investors and public economic planners alike. Local community associations, on the other hand, began to resent the high-priority attention that the High Line received in comparison to other rezoning proposals. Both civic and block associations had identified redevelopment priorities that included affordable housing projects, transportation improvements, and new outdoor parks and recreational facilities (Design Trust for Public Space, Conard, Smiley 2002). A local civic association member remarked, "The High Line is nice, but perhaps because of it we don't have all the other things that we need in this community" (Comstock 2009).

And, the FHL tried to have it both ways, trying to distance themselves from the zoning-related deals being struck all around the High Line. Those deals are likely what enabled the High Line park to exist at all. The West Chelsea rezoning was an attempt to reconcile development-based interests with the neighborhood focus of community residents. After all, both FHL cofounders live in the neighborhood and have for years.

Like the discourse around development, the negative and sour notes in discourse dealing with the neighborhood intensified over time, especially after Section One opened. This can be seen in the discussions surrounding the economic impact of the High Line in terms of investment in and around the High Line, including a focus on construction occurring in the West Chelsea and Meatpacking areas—new buildings and warehouse conversions, condominiums, hotels, galleries, and public spaces designed by big-name architects like Gehry, Nouvel, Meier, and Selldorf (Kershaw 2010). Since the High Line opened, over 2,500 new residential units, 1,000 hotel rooms and over 500,000 square feet of office and art gallery space have gone up in the neighborhood. The construction and related development has generated two billion U.S. dollars in private investment in the area, over 900 million U.S. dollars in increased taxes, and has created over 12,000 jobs (Quintana 2016). But, there has been more grumbling in the discourse around the High Line about who the two billion U.S. dollars benefit, who lives in the luxurious new buildings, and who has the new jobs created by the High Line (Budds 2016).

Some argue that the overall effect of the city's rezoning has created expensive, market-rate housing and has been middling at best in terms of affordable housing (Satow 2012). Some argue that the High Line created a real estate boom without any real benefits for the local community, claiming "[t]he High Line was a Trojan horse for the real-estate people" (Budin 2015). The buildings that the High Line's rezoning enabled will soon block out the air, light, and views that helped to win the park

Racial Composition of New York overall and high line census tracts, 2000 and 2010

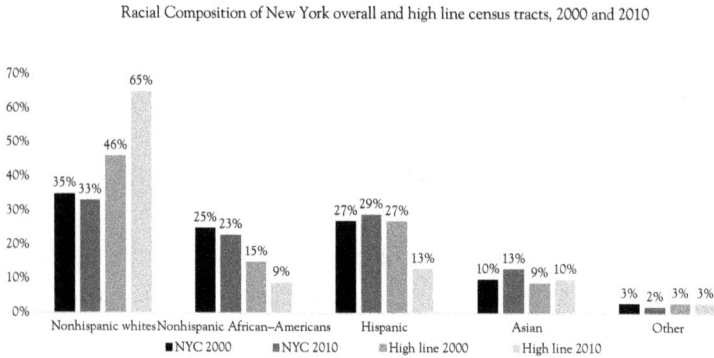

Figure 2.5 Population in High Line adjacent census tracts and New York City, by race, 2000 and 2010

Source: ACS Factfinder 2005–2009, NYC Department of Planning, Census 2000 and 2010.

awards and praise when its first section opened in 2009. It is probably worth imagining what things would be like if the High Line had not been accompanied by aggressive rezoning.

At the same time, the neighborhoods near the High Line[5] have seen a population increase from 28,000 to 42,000 in 10 years, an average annual increase of 4.07 percent. The neighborhood has also seen changes in racial composition and increased wealth. Figure 2.5 shows the demographic changes in the High Line area, compared to the New York City as a whole.

Individuals in the High Line census tracts make more money, on average, than individuals in Manhattan or New York City. Based on 2010 census data, the median household annual income for these census tracts is over 83,000 U.S. dollars, compared with nearly 69,000 U.S. dollars for Manhattan, as a whole. These 14,000 U.S. dollars are an income premium of approximately 21 percent. The income premium has significantly increased since the 2000 census, when the median household income for the High Line adjacent tracts was slightly over 54,000 U.S. dollars, compared with an average for Manhattan of 56,000 U.S. dollars. Since 2000,

---

[5] For purposes of situating the park, I use census tracts that are adjacent to the High Line. They are census tracts in Manhattan, numbered 83, 89, 93, 97, 99, 103, 111, 115, and 117 as of the 2010 census.

the area around the High Line has gone from being slightly less wealthy than Manhattan overall to significantly wealthier than Manhattan overall.

There is still a wide distribution of household income within the High Line adjacent tracts, including two low-income housing projects, and advocacy groups representing these areas are among those complaining about being left behind by the High Line-related development. Changes in the neighborhood have been reflected in the removal of long-time businesses in and around the High Line (Del Signore 2011; Budin 2015), and increasing complaints by newer residents of luxury buildings about the area's industrial businesses and services (Del Signore 2011). At a 2011 CUNY panel discussion, Hammond took pains to say that the High Line is not simply for the wealthy:

> most people think of Chelsea as just a very wealthy neighborhood. But, approximately, about 90 percent of the kids in the neighborhood are on a lunch program. You have two large, low income housing projects there. ... So it's an interesting gentrification issue, where you're not pushing people out that were right next to the High Line. But it's going to be a neighborhood of very wealthy and very poor. That's why a lot of our programs focus on the people in the neighborhood or actually all of our programs we try to focus on locals. (Hammond 2011)

Notably, the FHL has tried to engage with the community, and things have gotten a little better. In 2015, for example, about 31 percent of the park's total visitors—over 2 million people—were from New York City, with an additional 9 percent of visitors coming from within 45 miles of New York City. Diversity has also increased significantly since the park's early days. In 2015, 34 percent of High Line visitors were nonwhite, compared to 19 percent who identified as nonwhite in a survey FHL conducted in 2009 to 2010. Among the New York City residents who visited the High Line in 2015, 44 percent identified as nonwhite, compared with 24 percent in 2009 to 2010 (thehighline.org).

Despite Hammond's point, and the increased visitor diversity, the FHL has only been moderately successful in ensuring that long-time members of the community feel like the High Line also serves them.

Thanks to the High Line's popularity and continued neighborhood development, real-estate prices in the neighborhood have been steadily increasing. Chelsea space now rents for as much as 120 to 125 U.S. dollars per square foot, compared with 60 to 95 U.S. dollars per square foot in 2008 (Plitt 2015).

Others complain that the effects of the High Line are more limited than they expected or hoped for. When Section One of the High Line opened in 2009, critics raved while neighboring small businesses looked on uncertainly, hoping the park would be a rising tide to lift all boats. That did not happen. While small businesses hoped tourists would be good for the local economy, the tourists do not come down to the local neighborhoods. "They get off their big tour bus down at Gansevoort, walk to the end, and then the bus picks them up again. Most of them never get off the High Line" (Max, via Budin 2016). By the time the High Line opened in Section Two, in 2011, the small businesses in its shadow were dropping like flies, making room for massive, high-rise developments exclusively for the global super-rich.

In fact, FHL cofounder Hammond himself would now agree with those sentiments. In an interview with The Atlantic in 2017, Hammond said he and his co-founder were focused more on the aesthetics of the park, as they were planning it, than on the effect it would have on residents living around.

> Instead of asking what the design should look like, I wish we'd asked, 'What can we do for you? Because people have bigger problems than design....We were from the community. We wanted to do it for the neighborhood. Ultimately, we failed. (Bliss 2017)

It is easy to say that now, with the benefit of hindsight. To Hammond's credit, he has done more than simply express regret. He has created a network designed to help groups involved in this kind of adaptive reuse share resources, ideas, and best practices (http://network.thehighline.org/projects/). Notably, all of the other projects mentioned in this book are part of that network, along with groups in Washington D.C., Atlanta, Houston, Detroit, San Francisco, Queens, Dallas, Los Angeles, Toronto, Miami, Austin, and Seattle.

Summary and Conclusions: What They did Well or Less Well?

The FHL can be considered successful because, from 2000 to 2016, the FHL and its supporters consistently used several key themes in discussions about the High Line Park to build a deep and broad coalition of support from businesses bordering the park, city government agencies, and other interested organizations. The FHL used a combination of discursive techniques and media, including images, tours, in-person participation in municipal meetings (Community Board, City Council, and others), presentations, and interviews. By contrast, opposing voices were unsuccessful in their attempts to frame the discourse. Their efforts to develop themes were inconsistent, the types of media used in support of their arguments were much narrower, and were generally based on print interviews or in-person participation at Community Board and City Planning meetings.

The strongest themes were about how the park would look, how FHL would ensure it opened, and what the park could mean to the neighborhood. The venture had an air of curiosity—could these two guys, seemingly out of nowhere, actually pull it off? For their part, David and Hammond enjoyed the admiration they inspired as it became clear the High Line would open. They knew how to cultivate and maximize exposure and support.

Post-opening, there was a renewed focus on the park's aesthetic, an emphasis, though mixed in tone, on the development of the rest of the High Line and development occurring around the park, and somewhat negative messages about the relationship between the High Line and the surrounding neighborhoods. The mix of overwhelmingly positive discourse about the park's aesthetic and design with neutral or negative discourse about the resulting development and impact on the neighborhood, matters for how we see the venture's viability.

The increased focus on aesthetics may be the result of several factors. Given the initial support from the artistic and preservation communities and the role envisioning plays in a venture's viability, it is not surprising there was such emphasis on *what the park would look like*. In addition, as mentioned earlier, Section One of the park began to win awards for design and accolades for innovation. In terms of the park's development, while the park did partially open in 2009, plans to open the second section were continuing, and the third section had not yet been brought under city control. The FHL was simultaneously in operating and planning mode. And, the High Line's impact on the neighborhood was more dramatic and more mixed than predicted by FHL (David and Hammond 2011; Humm 2012; Budin 2015; Moss 2016).

To a certain extent, the success or failure of any public space depends on its ability to realize the imagination of its users. Neither the pre-project hype nor the post-hoc explanations or rationalizations could realistically be provable. But, the development of a consensus around these conclusions is interesting in and of itself. Observers can take issue with aspects of the park's design, but what makes the High Line's design concept breathtaking, and maybe even a little uncomfortable, is the kind of imagination it evokes. Hammond and David's key insight was to incorporate decades of neglect into the design fabric of the park, to make it something celebrating New York's forgotten industrial past (Bourne 2012; Plitt 2015).

In *Designing the High Line*, Robert Hammond described the sense of time passing, (Hammond 2008), arguing that observers could see what the High Line had been built for, and see how its moment was now gone. In a sense, the High Line embraces its neglected and decayed state of industrial ruin. Everywhere you look, you see that the neighborhood displays everything from the *old* Chelsea of parking lots and run-down brick facades to the restored cracked plaster and multimillion-dollar gardens made to look like neglected weed beds (thehighline.org, Bourne 2012; Kimmelman 2014).

Whatever else people say about the High Line, it is a creative response to a genuine social phenomenon and creates open space where none existed. It is also a more modest kind of public–private coalition, standing in stark contrast to "the model used in the '90s, and the early part of the 20th century, where when cities thought about large public/private partnerships, they invariably thought about sports stadiums" (Gladwell 2011). What you make of it depends on what you think of its underlying subject, which, in this case, is gentrification. If you are part of the community pushed out by the wealth gentrification brings, then what some see as the High Line's attention to symbols of industrial decay and historical ruin may seem annoying to you. If, on the other hand, you are part of a gentrifying wave, as so much of New York now is, you may delight in the distressed steel girders and exposed brick walls. Or, if you are an outside observer, you may think, as I do, that the High Line is a lovely place to spend a sunny day in New York.

CHAPTER 3

Friends of the 606: Building a Coalition to Build the Park

The 606 is currently the longest elevated greenway in the United States, a nearly three-mile long (12 acre), linear urban park. It is slightly more than 30 feet wide for most of its length, rising approximately 15 feet above the street level. The 606 includes the former Bloomingdale Line, an elevated railroad right-of-way on Chicago's northwest side comprised of reinforced concrete retaining walls, soil, and 37 bridges where it crosses other roads. The greenway cuts across dense residential neighborhoods (home to almost 250,000 residents), a light manufacturing district, major commercial streets, a rapid transit line, an eight-lane interstate highway, and a river.

The 606 runs through four different Chicago wards: the First, the 26th, the 32nd, and the 35th (www.bloomingdale606.org). The First Ward contains parts of Wicker Park and Humboldt Park and is primarily Hispanic. The 26th Ward also runs through Humboldt Park and is also primarily Hispanic. The 32nd Ward contains the 606-adjacent neighborhoods of Bucktown and Wicker Park, and is generally whiter and more affluent than the other wards. The 35th Ward contains parts of Logan Square and Humboldt Park and is more socioeconomically and demographically mixed than the other wards. Figure 3.1 shows the 606 relative to the Greater Chicago area.

The Friends of the 606, formerly known as the Friends of the Bloomingdale Trail (FBT), have been working on this project for over 15 years. They raised money from private donors and the federal government to complete the first phase of construction, which involved opening the entire 606 at a usable but low level of finish. With the dedicated help of the Trust for Public Land (TPL), the FBT is in the process of raising private money for the additional, decorative phase of construction. It has built a coalition of supporters, combining socially distinct neighboring

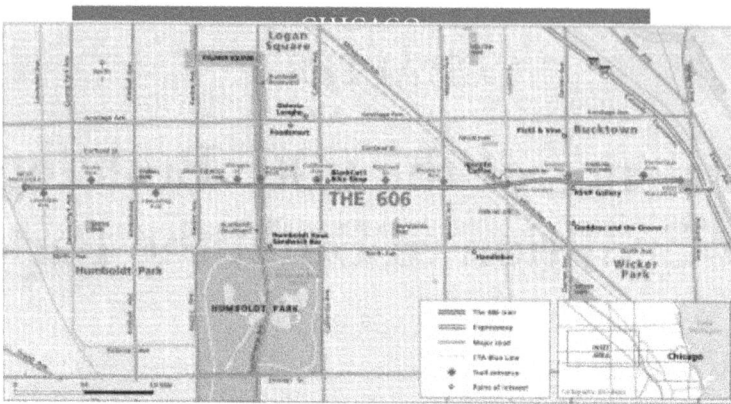

Figure 3.1 Bloomingdale trail or 606, Chicago
Source: 606.org

communities, government agencies, private donors, nonprofits, other interested local organizational actors, and so on. Their neighborhood support comes primarily from the communities of Logan Square, Bucktown, and Wicker Park. There has been little involvement by Humboldt Park community members, neither actively supporting it nor organizing against it.

The FBT and its supporters can be considered successful because they were able to develop and support several key themes around the 606 and development efforts, over time and across audiences. First, the FBT focused on emphasizing how users would access the 606 and what they would do once on the 606. The FBT also developed and maintained themes around how the 606 would be operated once open, and how the 606 would fit in with the disparate neighborhoods it connected. The presence of key themes and the consistency with which they are treated can be seen as a measure of FBT's ability to reconcile the competing logics they are drawing upon and frame their solution—the 606—as the correct one for the identified problem.

Brief History of Civic Action

In the early 2000s, as part of the City of Chicago's Open Space plan (City of Chicago et al. 2004; Stephen 2012), the city identified potential pockets of green space that could be developed in different city neighborhoods. In 2002, the City of Chicago and the Chicago Park District, an independent local governmental entity, began developing the Logan Square Open Space Plan. The plan listed 11 locations in the Logan Square area that if developed, would address the current deficiency in Logan Square's open park space acreage. That list included plans to convert the nearly three-mile long Bloomingdale Line into an elevated, multiuse, linear park and trail (Logan Square Open Space Plan Task Force 2004); the project eventually was named the 606, in honor of Chicago's area code. FBT was initially a group of Logan Square-based bike enthusiasts who began discussing the 606 and the prospect of developing it, as a result of attending community meetings. This group realized they needed to organize formally, to show support for development, and to backup this support with community-based planning.

In October 2002, as part of their work on the Open Space Plan, six members of the task force formed the formal entity then known as the FBT and now called The Friends of the 606 (Stephen 2012). Ben Helphand, the current President of FBT, was among them. These six individuals had backgrounds ranging from community organizing to operating small restaurants to community garden preservation (www.606.org). This group of six soon became a group of 20, and FBT was enthusiastically advocating for the conversion of the 606 embankment into an elevated, multiuse, linear park. The initial group of 20 people has swelled to over 1,000. Through organizing community events, FBT has strived to be the community's introduction to and voice for the vision of the 606. As Ben Helphand, FBT's president comments, our initial goals were, you know, "Preserve the right-of-way." What we found pretty quickly is pretty much everybody liked this idea, and nobody was actively against it. We visited all the community groups, made presentations, got official endorsements from all the local elected officials. So, very quickly [a] need to circle the wagons was irrelevant. And what we turned into is really more of a champion of this, keeping the wheels greased, keeping people excited about it, holding events, keeping the idea in the forefront of people's minds and imagination. And that has been our main focus over the years (Helphand 2009).

FBT has focused on building a coalition of partners to support 606's development. The leadership at FBT reached out to the national advocacy group Rails-to-Trails Conservancy (RTC) for help in the initial stages of advocacy, including asking RTC to help spread the word about the 606 to its membership and encourage them to attend public meetings (Oberg 2011; Helphand 2011). The Trust for Public Land (TPL), a national land conservation organization,[1] has taken a public leadership role in spearheading private fundraising, overall project development, and management of the 606.

TPL has worked on the 606 project since 2006, when the City of Chicago and the Friends of the 606 asked for assistance with land acquisition, community participation, and design competitions.[2] TPL and FBT created the 606 Collaborative as a framework for public and private sector partnerships to do the project. The collaborative has engaged nearly 25 organizations and agency departments; those most heavily involved are the Chicago Department of Transportation (CDOT), responsible for applying for Federal funding, the Chicago Department of Zoning and Land Use Planning (CZLUP), responsible for permitting and land acquisition for access parks, and the Chicago Park District (CPD), with ultimate operational and maintenance responsibility.[3]

In 2007, the Chicago Metropolitan Agency for Planning designated CDOT for federal transportation funding for design and engineering

---

[1] TPL is the nation's leader in creating parks and conserving land for people from the inner city to the wilderness. They are a national organization that is focused on urban public spaces in the form of city parks and playgrounds, urban gardens, and other green projects in and around cities, large and small.

[2] TPL, in its capacity as owner's representative for the Chicago Park District, is working with the Chicago Park District and two City departments: the Department of Transportation and the Department of Housing and Economic Development. Once the trail is complete, the Chicago Park District will assume ownership of the trail (tpl.org).

[3] In a unique arrangement with the city of Chicago, TPL is actually corralling all the local nonprofits, city agencies, donors, and railroad companies involved. The organization, which usually functions simply as a land trust, is also becoming the *agent* that manages the park over the long term.

work. In November 2008, the City of Chicago released a request for proposals to address the engineering analyses required in the preliminary design of the 606 (TPL, Winter 2008–2009). In June 2010, CPD's Board of Commissioners approved a challenge grant of up to 450,000 dollars to TPL, to coordinate the 606 Civic Engagement and Stewardship Project. Under the terms of the challenge grant, TPL expanded participation to additional community and civic organizations that expressed an interest in playing a role in the 606's development.

Most of the project's Phase One budget was covered by federal anti-congestion and air-quality funding federal funds (Chicago Metropolitan Agency for Planning 2011), and part of TPL's challenge grant involved a commitment to raise the remaining 20 percent of needed funds. But, even as the project was moving forward and design for Phase One had been awarded, there was not a clear sense of when the 606 would actually open (Vance 2009), until Mayor Rahm Emanuel was elected in 2011, and announced that the 606 would open by the end of his first term (Helphand 2011; White 2011). The first phase, which involved opening the entire park or elevated trail at a minimal finish level, opened in June 2015. Phase Two is underway, and there is not yet a definitive completion estimate.

Discourse Themes as Mechanism for Reconciling Competing Logics

The discourse is divided almost equally among the three dimensions of institutional work the 606 entrepreneurs have undertaken in order to make their project a reality, consistent in tone, and mostly neutral or positive. The only exception is the gentrification subtheme within the neighborhood theme, which is neutral or negative in tone. Table 3.1 summarizes the dominant themes within every dimension along with a note on the tone and consistency within each theme.

In addition to being tonally consistent, the discourse is relatively balanced over time, with each dimension accounting for approximately one-third of the discourse. Access or usability dominated the envisioning dimension. The development process dominated the creating dimension.

Table 3.1 Summary of themes within institutional dimensions in the 606 discourse

Dimension of institutional work	Theme	Tone of theme in discourse	Consistent use of theme in articles, interviews, discussions, and presentations
Envisioning	Access or usability	Neutral or positive	Yes
Envisioning	Aesthetic	Positive	Yes
Creating	Development	Neutral	Yes
Creating	FBT capacity	Neutral	Yes
Legitimating	Green	Positive	Yes
Legitimating	High Line	Neutral or Positive	Yes
Legitimating	History	Positive	Yes
Legitimating	Narrative	Positive	Yes
Legitimating	Neighborhood	Subtheme gentrification: neutral or negative Subtheme of safety-neutral or positive	Consistent within each subtheme, but split overall

The theme of neighborhood dominated the legitimating dimension. These three main themes together accounted for 73 percent of the coded discourse.

Envisioning Work

Access or usability comprised 27 percent of the overall discourse; most of the discourse around that theme is positive or neutral. The intersection of access and usability issues has come about because the 606 incorporates bicycles, requiring ramp-based access, and requiring complex kinds of development efforts to link the 606 and the ground. In addition, the entire 606 opened all at once, like the proposed Lowline, but unlike either the High Line Park in New York or the Rail Park in Philadelphia. Opening all at once affects both access and usability (Leopold 2011; Bornstein 2011; White 2011); all access points must be open (for ADA compliance reasons), as opposed to the High Line Park, which had initial access points designated for each section as it opened.

Figure 3.2 shows an image of a trail access point.

Figure 3.2 606, trail access point

Source: Victor Grigas/Wikimedia Commons/Bloomingdale Trail, the 606, Chicago 2015-35.jpg

Emphasizing how to access the space in the discourse around the 606 makes the project feel more tangible. If stakeholders are debating where to develop access parks, or how the access ramps should look, they have already bought in to the project happening. As with FHL in New York, this changes the entire discussion to one focused on "getting it done," as opposed to "should we do it?"

Even in the beginning stages of the project, it was clear that being able to experience the 606 and park at multiple levels was part of the appeal (Pietrusiak 2004; Dickhut 2011). Andrew Vesselinovitch, park's Director, Chicago Office, TPL, explained that "because this is elevated, unlike many parks, you need to be very conscious of where the entrance and exit points are going to be......there was a discussion of where these access points were gonna be. Many of them are existing parks" (Helphand and Vesselinovitch 2009). This inclusion of the ground-level parks as access points was partly driven by the fact that the ground-level parks could open before the elevated portion of the 606 (Helphand 2011; White 2011). In 2007 to 2008, once it became clear that the park was moving forward, and the city was intent on developing it as a park, discussions began to focus on how to access the park, as it was nearly 15 feet off the ground. As David Leopold, Chicago DOT Project Manager described,

> Our space is certainly similar [to the High Line] in terms of the idea of a lifted landscape. I think it's similar in terms of we use the old infrastructure for a new purpose that it wasn't originally intended for, but that these can have lives beyond the original intention. I think what's different, of course, is that ours is a multi-use path as opposed to more of a strolling environment.... certainly intended to be welcoming to bikes...[and] is a raised embankment; has a little more earth to it, with bridges crossing over various streets through the neighborhood and things like that. So .... I think it allows us to do different things that maybe the High Line would not have (Leopold 2011).

The team had to determine how the access points would be designed, and how the 606 would balance competing, possibly conflicting park uses. "There is a tension between is this a multi-use path that connects a group of parks? Or is it a park in itself?" (Bornstein 2011). The design team reached out to bring community members into the design process. They wanted to understand what members wanted the park and 606 to look like (even if not everything on the wish list was achievable). Part of this process involved a Fall 2011 charrette, where community members actively participated in discussions around the aesthetics of the 606 (Galef 2009; Vance 2011). It became clear from those discussions that community members wanted a park and multiuse trail, but feared conflict between people walking and biking (Dries 2012; Hauser 2017). They also found that that community members wanted many access points (October 2011 charrette meetings, Vance 2011).

As a result of the 606's narrow width, and based on community feedback, the design team decided to plan the elevated trail activities to serve individuals and small groups, instead of accommodating big gatherings.

The ground-level parks are designed to accommodate neighborhood uses such as playgrounds, basketball courts, skate parks, and access parks; this set of uses can enhance the relationship between the ground level and the elevated park (October 2011 charrette meetings, Vance 2011; Vance 2012).

Traditional park amenities, like large open spaces for large groups, ball fields, and play areas, are all things that would be hard to accommodate on a narrow trail, but can be accommodated in adjacent facilities. Many of the surrounding neighborhoods are communities of color; these kinds of common recreations draw people of color *in particular* to parks (Bliss 2017). Note that this positioning is in contrast to that taken by the Friends of the High Line (FHL) and supporters, who focused on the High Line as a beautiful open space as opposed to a park.

As bicyclists and pedestrians would both use the 606, questions surfaced about how to separate the two uses safely, and how the park would work for different segments of the neighborhood—who is it designed for? (Helphand and Vesselinovitch 2009; Hauser 2017). Notably, there are still questions about whether the space really works for both cyclists and pedestrians, with regular reports of pedestrians being struck by cyclists, in some cases causing serious injury (Hauser 2017). There were and still are feelings by some members of the community that the 606 has been designed for the cyclist community, *not* the Hispanic or minority community. The Hispanic or minority community has members who might use the 606 as a safe walk to school, and so on—the cycling community, far less so (October 2011 charrette meetings, Vance 2011; Gomez-Feliciano 2011; Echevarria 2011).

I …. acknowledge ADA access, and …. there would be access at least every half mile with a ramp so that it's accessible to everyone. … I have been suggesting that they put in place staircases in between every half mile….. And I think that is also going to help get more of the local people up—says Lucy Gomez-Feliciano, Health Issues Coordinator, Logan Square Neighborhood Association.

I think it has a potential to function as a park but that potential can only be realized to the degree that people see it as something that they own, something that's part of their community, their neighborhood. If people don't—you know if the residents don't use it then it will be relegated to merely a bike trail, says Raul Echevarria, Puerto Rican Cultural Center.

The usability discussion and programming were largely driven by the sources of funding. The choice of discourse themes is always constrained to some degree by the physical object: its location, its visual characteristics. As the first phase of the project was funded largely through Federal Congestion Mitigation or Air Quality (CMAQ) transportation funds, the 606 must accommodate cyclists as well as pedestrians (Leopold 2011; Chicago Metropolitan Agency for Planning 2011). Frankly, the cycling part of the 606 does explain, at least in part, the focus on access and usability themes in the envisioning discourse. "It was very helpful explaining to the public that it would have to accommodate bikes as well as people walking to the bus stop," Vesselinovitch said. "People understood that you can either allow bicycles or try to find [nearly] $40 million somewhere else" (Brake 2012). As a result of the programming requirements, there is a shared bike or pedestrian path running the length of the elevated part of the 606 as well as shorter, additional pedestrian-only segments along the wider portions. This programming requirement, plus the 606's narrow width, limits the amount and kind of plantings that the space can handle.

At a March 2012 public meeting, the design team unveiled a framework plan that responded to the October 2011 charrette. An important objective of this framework plan was to balance park aspirations. As Joseph Bornstein, from CPD, described it,

> some people think the 606 itself should be you know, like the High Line in New York. That the 606 itself will be decked out in the amazing every single inch of the way. Whereas others think, you know, there are parts where the 606 is a little wider where you can do some really cool things but for the most part it's going to be a 606, an elevated 606. And the fun parts will be pretty much just the parks along the way (Bornstein 2011).

A concession made to the pedestrians was the decision to limit cycling to no greater than 20 MPH (Chicago-pipeline.com, Vance 2012). It is not clear if this concession helps pedestrians (Hauser 2017), given the narrow space, and multiple, competing uses. A second concession, made to both bikers and walkers, was to pull back from plans for a "wheel-friendly event plaza" (Greenfield 2017) for biking and skating at an access park at the east end of the 606, in the Bucktown neighborhood. The official reason for leaving the existing area un-programmed is that nearby residents find the area lovely (Greenfield 2017), and it is located near a playground and dog-friendly area on the 606's north side. But, another motivation for leaving the area un-programmed appears to be the neighbors' negative perceptions of the skateboarders (mostly teenagers) who would have used the facility. The residents have not been completely silent on this issue. "Skateboarders bring in a different element to [The] 606 than bicyclists, walkers and joggers" (Hauser 2017), not one residents necessarily want to see. Figure 3.3 shows an unprogrammed access park.

Figure 3.3 Un-programmed access park
Source: Google Street View.

Creating Dimension-Development or Cost

The discourse in this dimension has to explain why FBT, as the community voice for the 606, makes sense as a solution to the problem FBT has identified and reframed. The dominant theme in this dimension was the overall process of 606 development and associated costs. Most of the discourse is positive or neutral. Negative messages within this theme start off at about the same level as neutral themes, but quickly become less prevalent in the discourse, starting in 2005 to 2006. Negative themes became stronger again when the project was under development for several years without much momentum.

The discourse and dialog around development of the 606 fell into two broad subthemes, due to the extended nature of the 606's development process. On the neutral or negative side, journalists and bloggers expressed skepticism over whether the project would actually happen, despite the city's support. On the positive side, the process enabled the Friends of the 606 to define and refine their role, and allowed city government agencies, TPL, and FBT to explain, consistently, the roles of different network partners in the 606's development coalition along with framing the cost as an investment in the area.

TPL began highlighting the role of the FBT while discussing the 606's possibilities in its quarterly newsletters (TPL, Winter 2006; Summer 2007; Winter 2007–2008), with particular focus on the access parks needed to link the 606 to the ground. Ground-level access parks were a critical part of the 606, and because they were actually developable ahead of the 606 itself, those parks became the TPL's main focus (TPL.org, White 2011; Helphand 2011; Oberg 2011; Ciabotti 2011) Both FBT and TPL felt that opening the parks would increase awareness of the project and provide much-needed green space for the four communities surrounding the 606. Using its own money sources as well as fundraising, TPL helped the City of Chicago to acquire four city lots needed to access the 606 (activelivingbydesign.org 2007), though the city has ownership and maintenance responsibility. Their efforts were reported in the local papers, along with their investment in the 606. "So far, the Trust has spent $2 million buying properties to be used for access to the elevated 606" (Dominick 2008, also see TPL Winter 2007–2008). TPL and FBT also highlighted private, corporate donors involved in supporting the new parks.

> Foundations giving money to BT: Alcoa, Local Initiatives Support Corporation (LISC), New Communities Program, MetLife, Oberweiler Foundation, Dr. Scholl, Related Midwest, Gaylord and Dorothy Donnelley Foundation, and Searle Funds at the Chicago Community Trust. (TPL, Winter-2007–2008)

The contract for Phase One development was awarded in 2009 to a multicompany construction and development group led by Michael Van Valkenburgh Associates (Greenfield 2010; Vance 2011). While the design team began to develop detailed construction drawings, estimates for the park's cost began to increase. Initial estimates put the 606 at 20 million dollars (Pietrusiak 2004). By 2011, estimates had quadrupled (tpl.org 2010; Greenfield 2011). Some of this increase can be attributed to better information about the kind of work required to convert the structure to a park, including completed engineering studies, and thus the condition (and any repair work required) of all 37 bridges along the 606 (White 2011; Bornstein 2011). Some of it can be attributed to increasing the scope of work, including plantings. Some of it can be attributed to developing the access parks.

Of the total amount needed for construction, 46 million dollars was dedicated to Phase One and the remainder to Phase Two (Kamin 2011). Phase One, or *Basic* (Dries 2012), opened the complete 606 system and access points to the public. Phase Two focuses on building and sprucing up existing parks next to the 606, including walkways, architectural flourishes, and public art, as well as providing for long-term maintenance (Donovan 2012). These estimates do not include at least two million dollars in land acquisition costs (activelivingbydesign.org 2007).

City agencies, FBT, and TPL all had to explain the project's increasing price tag and delays in building despite the apparent support. There were concerns that Chicago, as cash-strapped as it was, would have to shoulder most of the construction cost (Kamin 2011). In response, the team had to explain that Phase One was funded largely through Federal CMAQ transportation funds, so the Federal government provided much of the funds, and that money just takes longer to get (Pietrusiak 2004; Fagel 2009; Bornstein 2011; Leopold 2011; Chicago Metropolitan Agency for Planning 2011). Part of the delay in construction was also due to the fallout from the 2008 economic slowdown, projects just taking longer to be approved, and new administrations in both Washington, DC and the City of Chicago. As Joseph Bornstein of the Chicago Park District explained:

> To get to why can't you just start building it now and why does it need to take that long? I've always found—and please do not let

this come across as condescending but—people who don't work in industries where you build things never understand how difficult it is to get all your approvals and do all your steering and as well to line up all the necessary funding for something. (Bornstein 2011)

City officials consistently said not everything people want aesthetically in the 606 will be there, due to funding limitations and the pressure to open the 606 all at once. Chris Gent, the Park Liaison from the Cultural Affairs Department said, "It's a very different and unique space but not everything can be accommodated" (Gent 2011). Kathy Dickhut, from the Department of Zoning and Land Use Planning, concurred, saying that

I'm sure we can get something open from end to end that's safe, that's usable, that's interesting.... Will it include everything everybody's thought about and everybody wants? Probably not, but that doesn't mean that over time things can't be sort of embellished. (Dickhut 2011)

Some of the demands for certain items or activities that could not be accommodated came about as a result of the community-visioning sessions FBT organized throughout the long development process. There are many members of the communities affected by the 606 who faithfully came to and participated in community-visioning sessions, over a period of years, and *kept the faith*, so to speak. As a result, they developed a belief that expressing a particular vision over years and years, even without funding and clear plans for the park, somehow made that vision more likely to be implemented. FBT wanted community members to buy in all along, but sometimes individuals get bought-in to what they have expressed, and for budgetary or other reasons, it is not possible to accommodate those demands. That can leave community members feeling cheated or affect their motivation. There is also an aesthetic challenge, given the high level of finishes of the High Line, a *sister project* of the 606, which notably opened in complete phases two to three years apart.

Focusing on the development process, and particularly FBT's role in keeping the community believing the 606 would happen, reassures community members and potential donors that the advocacy group involved, and advocacy, in general, can actually make the project happen. FBT also developed and touted the consistent theme that minimal City of Chicago taxpayer money was involved. Making sure community members know that most of the money required for Phase One came (theoretically) from Federal coffers worked to dampen project opposition.

Legitimating Dimension: Neighborhood

The final part of the discourse around the 606 involved connecting the supporting rationales of the project to the neighborhood. Notably, there was not very much discussion about the High Line, even though that was the only similar project in the United States open during planning. From talking with the individuals involved, the FBT coalition was afraid that explicitly using the High Line's words and phrases would have made their project appear elitist. Within the overall theme of the neighborhood, two different subthemes emerged. The first, by far the most dominant, involves issues of safety and security for neighborhood residents. The second involves the effects the 606 will have on gentrification, especially in the Western communities, and affecting long-time residents. This concern about gentrification appears in all four cases profiled.

Legitimating or Neighborhood Safety and Security

There are no bathrooms on the 606 or any of the access parks (3-8-12 Public meeting, 606.org), although there are plans to add public bathrooms to the McCormick YMCA, which provides an access point to the 606 (Bloom and Hauser 2017). A lack of bathrooms in the design limits opportunities for homeless people to linger on the 606, limits opportunities for general sexual predation or whatever,[4] and limits use of the 606 by nonresidents. So, FBT and its supporters sent a clear message that they were encouraging neighborhood 606 use. This is a clear contrast to the High Line project in New York, where "the High Line is one of a kind, but it wasn't designed to have accommodating neighborhood residents as

---

[4] A popular anti-homeless prejudice.

one of its guiding principles" (Stone 2012). It remains to be seen what happens once the bathrooms actually open, sometime in 2018.

The neighborhood safety theme is where there was the most disagreement in the discourse. City officials and supporters of the project all felt strongly that residents would be much safer once the 606 was converted for park use. One of the ways to manage community members' insecurity is to encourage as much use as possible and have many people up there (Gent 2011; Hauser 2017). Members of FBT have also emphasized that the 606 is close to 12 elementary schools; so the immediate community can use the 606 as a Safe Walk to School®. FBT and its supporters see increasing the diversity of users as increasing safety overall. This sentiment is very much in line with Jane Jacobs' concept of eyes on the street (Jacobs 1961); the 606, like a street, is safer when more people are on it. TPL estimates over 1.8 million people will use the 606 in 2017 (Hauser 2017).

At a 2012 public meeting, Glenn Brettner from the United Block Club of West Humboldt Park and a member of the Humboldt Park Advisory Council, also argued that, "I do not see ... that this will be less safe. There will be more people and more lighting which tends to lessen not increase crime" (Coorens 2012, 3-8-12 Public meeting). And, FBT President, Ben Helphand, insists that "the only long-term solution to crime is the 606 itself; anything we can do to hasten its creation will bring permanent safety to that corridor" (Helphand 2011). This position has been supported by the police, who describe crime on the 606 as really modest, (Hauser 2017), and urge continued use. "The safest thing we can do as a community is use it, stay on it. The more people on it, the better" (Hauser 2017).

Residents expressed concerns that people would be able to look right in their windows and be using the 606 until late at night,[5] acknowledging the tension between addressing the desire for privacy and also having *eyes on the 606*. While making the 606 into a park patrolled by police would make it safer overall, it also brings more people up onto the 606. In theory, this would mean more people who could look right into their homes, including the police.

---

[5] Chicago parks close at 11 pm.

Overall, crime has gone down since the 606 opened. In 2017, three researchers published a study comparing city crime statistics in neighborhoods closest to the 606 with similar socioeconomic neighborhoods elsewhere in Chicago. They compared crime statistics from 2011 to 2015, and found that all kinds of crimes fell faster in 606-adjacent neighborhoods than elsewhere (Bloom 2017). But, over the 16 months, including all of 2016 and the first seven months of 2017, there were 26 crimes reported on the trail, itself (Hauser 2017; Hauser 2017; Hauser 2017); at least a quarter of the crimes happened after 10:30 p.m., near or after the park's 11 p.m. closing time. Another quarter occurred between midnight and noon. The remaining half were between noon and 10:30 p.m. Those crimes feel like a lot, even though:

> When asked by a resident if he thinks the crime level is high or low, Sgt. Adam Henkels (CPD) responded: "really modest." Capt. Thomas Shouse (CPD) added that while "even one [crime is too many]," given the fact the [elevated part of the 606] is "basically the size of a beat but stretched out and up in the air, it's fairly low." (Hauser 2017)

Legitimating or Neighborhood Gentrification

Both the Humboldt Park and Logan Square areas have already seen demographic shifts, bringing more affluent whites into their communities and displacing long-time, primarily Hispanic, residents. In the past 10 years, the area around the 606 has become more White and less Hispanic, while the group of census tracts as a whole has seen almost no change in overall population. As Figure 3.4 shows, in 2000, the overwhelming majority of people living in census tracts near the 606 were Hispanic, but this number dropped substantially over the following decade.[6]

---

[6] For purposes of situating the park, I used 20 census tracts, all in Cook County that are adjacent to the 606. They are census tracts 2301, 2302, 2303, 2308, 2309, 2401, 2402, 2403, 2404, 2405, 2406, 2407, 2408, 2409, 2410, 2411, 2412, 2413, 2414, 2415, and 2416 (ACS 2005-2009, American Fact Finder (www.census.gov).

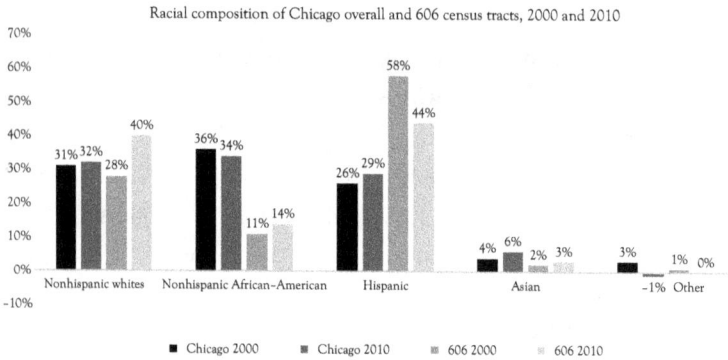

Figure 3.4 606-adjacent census tracts and Chicago total population, 2010 and 2000, by race

Source: American Community Survey, City of Chicago GIS.

Median household annual income for these 20 census tracts is approximately 52,350 dollars, compared with 46,781 dollars for Chicago overall. This income premium is approximately 12 percent, and household income has increased an average of 3.6 percent annually since 2000, when it was slightly over 36,000 dollars for the 606-adjacent census tracts (www.census.gov). In addition, housing prices in the Humboldt Park, Logan Square, and Wicker Park or Bucktown neighborhoods increased by 21.5, 13.5, and 9.2 percent, respectively, in the first year since the 606 opened (Institute for Housing Studies 2017), compared with 8 percent for the City of Chicago overall. More specifically, there has been a 50 percent surge in home prices since 2013, when construction on the project began. The most dramatic increases have hit the trail's less affluent west end, in the Humboldt Park and Logan Square neighborhoods (Jacobs 2017).

The concerns of long-time area residents would seem to accurately reflect the changes in their neighborhoods and the people around them. In early 2017, two local Aldermen introduced legislation designed to slow down the pace of gentrification near the 606 through zoning changes or developer incentives or fines (Bloom and Hauser 2017). It may be too little too late—the 606 had been in the works for several years before it was completed and arguably the Aldermen should have anticipated the problems (Schulte 2017).

FBT has had mixed success in understanding the Humboldt Park and Logan Square communities, and in encouraging real participation. This has become more problematic as Logan Square has gentrified. Yes, a lot of planning has happened, yet the plan of outreach to said communities and the surrounding residents (houses, homeowners, organizations, block clubs, churches) right next to the 606 never really turned into resident support. As a result, project support has come primarily from the East and North sections of the 606, and there has been scattered support from other segments of the community. Former FBT Board Member and community activist Raul Echevarria said he thinks it is partly to do with how FBT members have been used to organizing the whiter, more affluent parts of the 606 community.

> This is very much a Logan Square driven project and … they sort of have a way of working that is not—that was not really in line, in alignment with Humboldt Park….And so they struggled with it. [I had] some frustration just in maintaining that this is not working, using the same organizing [approach from Logan Square is] not gonna work in Humboldt Park. It's not gonna be just—it can't just be white male driven…. I mean they tried to make adjustments but it was just too much…it was just too much work you know to build beyond … their… way of working. (Echevarria 2011)

Further, Echevarria, and another Latinx former FBT Board Member (and community activist), Lucy Gomez-Feliciano, argued that FBT's bilingual fliers were not enough to address the cultural differences between the communities. "They have to ask themselves why don't people come to meetings?" (Echevarria 2011; Gomez-Feliciano 2011). Other examples of minority outreach include organized events underneath the 606's viaducts, and active recruitment for the community visioning sessions and charrettes. Gomez-Feliciano pointed out that, if FBT members just sent "it [the notice of the charrette] out to their friends it would not include a lot of the brown population in that community. …So, you know, I reached out to people to make sure that the people attending those charrettes are diverse" (Gomez-Feliciano 2011). But, Echevarria challenged her efficacy in getting participation, arguing that:

I think the only way that it would just really work [with] the local park is just with me or someone like me were driving those components in Humboldt Park. And other folks on the board, ….there was a Latina on the board [Lucy Gomez-Feliciano] but she was from Logan Square, [and I] think that she was also for buying a Logan Square way of doing things. She would not—she was not that successful. (Echevarria 2011)

Echevarria and Gomez-Feliciano gave the impression that the Humboldt Park and Logan Square residents are not against the 606 in concept, but may be against how it has materialized. There is not an organic grouping of Humboldt Park and Logan Square residents who want to put their time and energy into the 606 (Echevarria 2011); tellingly, there is also not an interest in organizing opposition to the 606. It is possible that many members of this less-affluent community really do not have the time to invest on either side of the project. Interestingly, both Echevarria and Gomez-Feliciano left the FBT Board due to changing job responsibilities. Gomez-Feliciano has continued to do outreach for the project through local community group Logan Square Neighborhood Association (LSNA). Echevarria does not do 606 outreach in his role, as his responsibilities as the Executive Director of the Puerto Rican Cultural Center take up most of his time.

Promoting the idea that the 606 is for the neighborhood does not completely resonate with some communities nor does it alleviate their concerns. Frankly, it cannot do that, given that the neighborhoods on the 606's Western side are changing. It is not entirely clear, here, which is the chicken and which is the egg. Is the park exacerbating existing demographic changes already going in Humboldt Park or Logan Square or would those changes happen anyway? Similar questions are being asked in New York, where gentrification has occurred around the High Line, and Lowline, as well as in Philadelphia. And, like in New York's High Line (and the proposed Lowline), there are times when part or all of the park is closed for a private event. While little private money was used to fund Phase One, which opened the whole trail, private fundraising is needed for Phase Two, which is more aesthetic. The Park District's involvement has also enabled them to close off parts of the 606 for fundraising dinners and special events (Hauser 2017). The event fees collected "help fund neighborhood park improvements and programs" (Tostado, via Hauser 2017). The closure of part (or all) of these parks for events again raises questions about who these parks are for, and the role of private money in public spaces.

Summary and Conclusions: What They Did Well and Less Well

FBT and its coalition of supporters raised enough to open the entire 606 Trail in *Basic* mode in June 2015. The choices they made along the way have resulted in a lovely, local, urban amenity very different in feel from New York's High Line. Unlike the High Line, there are few places to sit and linger along the 606's 2.7 miles. "The main focus is on movement... [since the] structure is typically only 32 feet wide." (White, quoted in Keegan 2015). That narrow width was a major design obstacle, and may become 606's biggest challenge. It might be a great place to bike and run and a terrible place to stroll—or it might be the opposite. It will only be a success if people can figure out how to interact based on different modes, and speeds, of transport along the way (Keegan 2015). Some argue that the 606 falls short of the High Line, in that it is "not a project of citywide significance, nor a bona fide tourist attraction for the masses. It's a neighborhood-serving rail-trail that is elevated above the streets with some nice features, like lighting, that you don't see often." (Greenfield 2015).

I disagree. The 606 may never be the tourist attraction the High Line is, and that is fine. The 606 draws people from many different parts of Chicago, and differs in three major ways from New York's amenity. First, it's nearly twice as long as the 1.45-mile Manhattan path. Second, unlike the High Line, you can bike on the Bloomingdale, and it provides direct access to 12 public and private schools, so it functions as a very useful transportation link and connector.

Finally, the 606 is more demographically democratic. The High Line runs through some of New York's most expensive real estate, and at least during the times I have visited, the crowd seemed to be homogenous. The 606 does exactly what it is designed to do; it connects economically and ethnically diverse neighborhoods; in nice weather, you can see whole working-class families, including grandparents and little kids, out on the 606. That is a sight you probably would not come across in Chelsea. About 1.6 million people used the 606 in its first full year of operation, a number projected to increase 15 percent in 2017 (Hauser 2017).

Some Chicagoans have argued that the city spent too much money to make the 606 a world-class amenity, while a simple paved path might have had similar benefits, with less impact on gentrification (Greenfield 2015). Others argue that the trail had "a budget that was too low, and the unfinished metal for railings and security fences along The 606 gives the trail a prison yard vibe; a design choice due to funding limitations" (Renn 2015). But, the trail itself is still largely a work in progress.

During the buildup to opening, Friends of the 606 and its coalition of supporters gave nearly equal time to each dimension of institutional work through active investment in the discourse. Each of the three dimensions plays a necessary role in seeing the venture through. Success or failure of the 606 depends on the ability of the advocacy group and its coalition to focus and bring to life the imagination of its potential users (and donors).

FBT and its supporters chose to focus on the practical aspects of the park's development. Ben Helphand argues that was purposeful, as "we want the Park to reflect that 'Chicago is the City' that Works" (Helphand 2011). That may be due to programming requirements and budget limitations, it may be post-hoc justification, or it may be an accurate reflection of the underlying attitude. That said, there is not a lot of discussion about the beauty or magic of the 606, as opposed to the discourse seen both in the High Line (discussed in Chapter 2) and the Rail Park (discussed in Chapter 4). Those elements are just less important in the discourse around the 606. The plan was always to get the 606 in functional shape as early as possible, and then raise money for more plantings and public art, plus recreational equipment for the access parks, as well as maintenance and programming. Of the 40 million dollars needed from private donations, 24 million dollars have been raised so far (Greenfield 2015).

In effect, FBT has treated the 606 and access parks as symbolic and physical opportunities to connect four neighborhoods: Humboldt Park, Logan Square, Bucktown, and Wicker Park. This strategy appears mostly to have worked in smoothing over racial or neighborhood-based tensions. That, itself, is an important achievement, given the different socioeconomic statuses of the four communities surrounding the park. Beth White of TPL has described the 606 and park combination as being a charm bracelet, with the parks dangling off the chain of the 606 (White 2011; Kamin 2011; Donovan 2012). Another way to think of it is that FBT has been able to use the 606 as the charm bracelet, and the communities as the charms, in its reconciliation of different, yet critical institutional logics.

CHAPTER 4

The Philadelphia Story: Huge Potential, Missed Chances

After more than a decade of effort, Philadelphia's Friends of the Rail Park (RPP) has made little progress toward repurposing the three-mile remnant passenger and freight train track known as the Rail Park into a public urban green space. While city government officials have indicated their support for the project, the city currently owns only 2.4 miles of the proposed three-mile space, with the rest remaining under private ownership by the entertainment company Reading International. Some money has been raised for construction of Phase 1, which involves developing a 0.25 mile section accessible at grade. No timeline exists for the other sections. The Friends of the Park group has an unclear role in the development of the Rail Park. Parts of the community are excited about the possibilities and other parts of the community are organized in opposition, seeing parts of the structure as blight literally hemming them in.

The Rail Park, if completed, would connect 10 Philadelphia neighborhoods, through 55 city blocks, using the tracks of the old Reading Railroad (Burnley 2016). The park runs both below-ground and aboveground; this combination is unique among the four cases profiled. The below-ground part of the route is in a former trench. The elevated parts use track built in the 1890s, on a combination of embankment sections bridged by steel structures and arched masonry bridges. The elevated parts of the structure also offer spectacular views of both the immediate neighborhoods and the Philadelphia skyline. Figure 4.1 shows the Rail Park in its proposed form.

The 501c(3) group known as the RPP has used discourse and presentation since 2003 to make the case for the abandoned tracks and trench

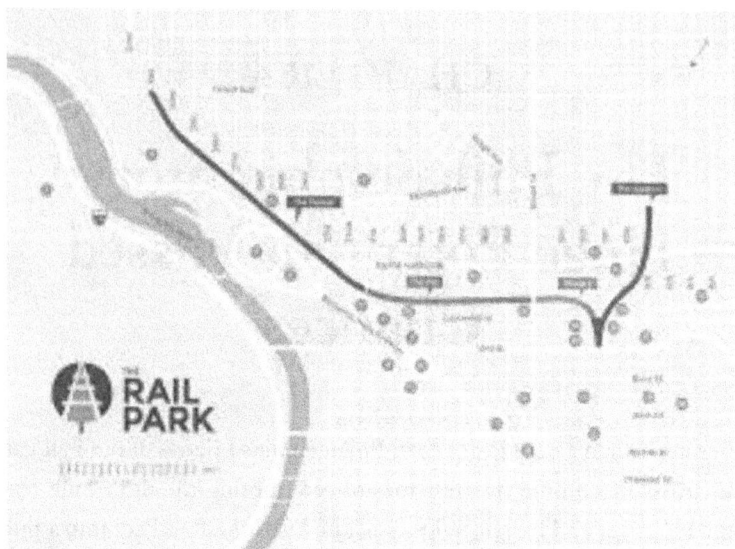

Figure 4.1 Rail Park, proposed form
Source: The Rail Park.

to be repurposed as an elevated linear park. They have not yet been able to build a broad coalition of support among community members, private foundations, wealthy philanthropists, and government agencies. The fragmentation found throughout the discourse around the park is linked to RPP's inability to reconcile the competing intuitional logics being applied and to frame their solution as the correct one for the identified problem.

Brief History of Civic Action

Efforts to redevelop the Rail Park have been in process for nearly 15 years. Initially, the Callowhill Neighborhood Association (CNA) advocated for development, inspired by the grassroots efforts of the Friends of the High Line in New York. In 2003, Sarah McEneaney and John Struble of the CNA helped found the Reading Viaduct Project (RVP) as a community group dedicated to the preservation and adaptive reuse of the abandoned, elevated, 0.86-mile Reading Viaduct. At the end of 2003, RVP held its first meeting as a dedicated nonprofit with 25 neighbors and concerned citizens.

Since 2003, the group's advocacy efforts have mostly consisted of giving tours of the site, giving presentations about the site, or taking city officials and other interested parties to see New York's High Line, approximately two hours away. The group has not really engaged with either the Trust for Public Land or the Rails-to-Trails Conservancy—two large and well-known entities involved in other similar projects, including Chicago's 606—in attempting to build a broader coalition to develop the Viaduct (Ciabotti 2011; Stone 2012; van Meter 2012).

In addition to funding constraints, the limited efforts of RPP may be due partly to the advocacy group's history and the complicated nature of site ownership. From 2011 to 2013, a competing group, Viaduct Greene, advocated for a larger and competing project, incorporating the elevated Viaduct into a three-mile running and biking trail crossing 55 city blocks (Burnley 2016). The two groups eventually merged in 2013 to form RPP (Popkin 2013), which is the entity currently advocating for the larger project.

The park's three sections are known as the Viaduct, the Cut, and the Tunnel. The mass transit authority Southeastern Pennsylvania Transportation Authority (SEPTA), a Philadelphia city government entity, owns both the Cut and the Tunnel, approximately 2.4 miles of the space. The international movie theater operator Reading International, the Reading Railroad's former operator, owns the remainder, shown as the Viaduct section in Figure 4.1 (McEneaney 2011; Edelstein 2011).

Several times, Reading International and the City of Philadelphia attempted to negotiate a transfer of ownership of the elevated Viaduct section from the company to the city. Each time, Reading offered to pay for part of the environmental cleanup required as part of the transfer, but the city government was in transition and unable to complete the negotiations.

In 2000 they made an offer where they would give us, you know, a large amount of money and the [section] to walk away. And we didn't respond because we were switching mayors and it was just a big mess… In 2004, [Reading] made another offer for less money. It was $500,000 to donate the [section] and walk away. (Edelstein 2011)

The project seemed to gain momentum in 2010, once Paul Levy of Center City District (CCD)[1] became an active supporter. Levy is well-known throughout Philadelphia and respected by members of city government for his work in cleaning up the downtown neighborhood of Center City. In 2010, CCD began working with both the RPP and the city's Departments of Commerce and Parks and Recreation to review the site's history and evaluate development options. CCD was drawn into the project by RPP co-founders McEneaney and Struble, and Levy described the experience of walking on New York's High Line as the key factor that changed his mind:

> For years people were talking about the [Viaduct portion] as a connector...I kept saying "it connects nothing to nothing. It's a stub now and it runs through a weak neighborhood." But two years ago I saw the High Line and it changed my perspective. Philadelphia is a gridded city and the [elevated Viaduct section] cuts at an angle across the streets and gives you a completely unusual perspective on the downtown skyline....I began to say, "this is not a connecting path. It is an anchor space for revitalizing the core of the city." (Levy 2011)

In May 2011, the city of Philadelphia entered into a third round of serious talks with Reading International to determine how to transfer ownership of the portion they own. However, with the opening of New York's High Line, Reading International's view of the project evolved as well. As David Edelstein put it:

> Now, essentially, … they want us to pay for it. …They evolved into an entertainment-related industry and company, … and then they have these kind of railroad legacy assets that they kind of mention in passing as a liability. And—I mean, that's what's particularly frustrating to us 'cause [sic] you know, they don't acknowledge that they have any value on their balance sheets, but you know, they're acting as if they do have a lot of value and they expect to do something with them. (Edelstein 2011)

---

[1] The CCD is a powerful neighborhood improvement district organization.

The current focus of RPP and its supporters is on development of a 0.25-mile spur, accessible at grade, and already owned by the city. The idea is to use that spur as a proof of concept, build momentum, and encourage Reading International to transfer ownership of the remaining parcel to the city. In 2011, with a new round of foundation grants, CCD, partnered with the city and commissioned a schematic design by Studio Bryan Hanes and Urban Engineers, focusing on the smaller, SEPTA-owned spur. They also conducted some community surveys to determine preferences. In March 2012, the team incorporated the preferences from the limited survey work and produced a series of renderings. The cost of the schematic alternative selected was estimated to be 6 to 8 million dollars (Popkin 2012). Construction on the portion accessible at ground level began in mid-2017, although funding for construction of that portion remains incomplete (Kopp 2017), and no overall timeline has been created for the combined project.

Themes in Discourse as Mechanism for Reconciling Competing Logics

This project's discourse was the hardest to track and code, because of the competing group, because the advocacy group changed its name and rebranded twice, and because supporters were not consistent in talking about the project. The dominant theme in the envisioning dimension was aesthetics or design, with 25 percent of the discourse. In the creating dimension, the development process dominated, with 18 percent of the discourse. In the legitimating discourse, the neighborhood, with 24 percent of the discourse, was the dominant theme. These three main themes together accounted for 68 percent of the coded discourse. Table 4.1 summarizes the dominant themes within every dimension along with a note on the tone and consistency within each theme. The discourse is inconsistent, ranging from negative to neutral or positive.

Given the project's long development history, it is also important to examine how the themes developed over time. There is an emphasis on the creating discourse early, on and later, the legitimating discourse becomes more dominant. Even since 2008 to 2009 (concurrent with the High Line's Section One opening), the discourse around the elevated Viaduct section, in particular, has been mostly neutral or negative. The following

Table 4.1 Summary of themes within institutional dimensions in the Rail Park discourse

Institutional work dimension	Theme	Tone of theme in discourse	Consistent use of theme in articles, interviews, discussions, and presentations
Envisioning	Access or usability	Neutral	Moderately. There was disagreement about what the park would actually be and that affected the consistency of the discourse
Envisioning	Aesthetic	Negative when talking about the blight of the abandoned elevated portion Positive when talking about the potential	No, extremely fragmented
Creating	Development	Neutral or negative	No, extremely fragmented
Creating	Coalition or RPP	Neutral	No, moderately fragmented
Legitimating	Green	Neutral or positive	Yes
Legitimating	High Line	Neutral or positive	No
Legitimating	History	Neutral or positive	Yes
Legitimating	Neighbor-hood	Negative when talking about Chinatown's views of the elevated Viaduct section Positive when talking about the potential to revitalize some blighted neighborhoods	Consistent within each subtheme, but strongly split overall
Legitimating	Opponent	Negative	Yes

section explores the dominant theme in each dimension. In addition, I explore two secondary themes—access to usability in the envisioning dimension and the High Line in the legitimating dimension. Both secondary themes support my contention that the overall discourse around the Rail Park is fragmented and affects the venture's viability.

Envisioning

One of the continuing challenges faced by the RPP is the inability to create a consistent mental picture of the project in the minds of potential supporters; visual objects can (and often do) carry unintended messages (Meyer et al. 2013). While the aesthetics or design theme dominated and most of the discourse was positive, the discourse was also incomplete and fragmented regarding the project. This pattern of gaps and fragmentation held over time, and there was also a negative theme that was well-organized. I also considered the theme of access or usability because the fact that the RPP and its supporters disagree about park use, worsens the fragmentation found elsewhere in the discourse.

Envisioning: Aesthetics

What the space should look like is different from how it should be used, though the concepts are related. The discourse around the aesthetics of the space has fallen into two broad categories: those who saw it as blight and those who saw it as an opportunity. The language around blight and related terms came from Center City residents living in Chinatown, the ethnic advocacy group Philadelphia Chinatown Development Corporation (PCDC), and their supporters.

Casting the elevated portion, or Viaduct, as blight has been an entrenched element in the discourse since 2008. RPP and its supporters cast the space in terms of the vistas, opportunities, and differences from other, urban environments expressed in an attempt to combat the image of the Viaduct as blight. In 2004, graduate students in the University of Pennsylvania School of Design participated in an intense, four-day-long charrette to develop concepts for the reuse of the structure (Rosof and Fallon 2004; Wilner 2004; Goldin 2007).

At the time, it seemed as if the charrette's ideas could have spurred project momentum. RPP co-founder McEneaney was quoted as saying she was hoping, with city support and prodding, that the railroad would pay for remediation (Rosof and Fallon 2004). However, 2004 also marked the release of the Chinatown Neighborhood Plan, developed over a two-year period. This planning process was coordinated by the Delaware

Valley Regional Planning Commission (DVRPC), and developed by the design firm Kise, Straw Kolodner (KSK), involving 17 different stakeholder groups, including PCDC, Asian Americans United (AAU), and CNA, even including RPP cofounders Struble and McEneaney (Heller 2009).

The 2004 neighborhood plan described a community that has slowly been hemmed into the south. In this case, the physical hemming in of Chinatown's residents, particularly by outside forces, had led to feelings of being hemmed in, under siege, and cut off. Additionally, Chinatown experienced rising residential prices, which created pressures to expand, encouraging the community to look north, to Callowhill, in particular the site of the Viaduct, for expansion and relief.

The 2004 development report called for the teardown of at least part of the Viaduct. Chinatown residents consider the decaying Viaduct structure dark, dirty, ugly, unsafe, a blight on their neighborhood, and an impediment to much-needed housing development (Gradinger 2004; Wilner 2004; DcnPhilly 2010). Unlike the consistent language on blight emanating from the PCDC and others, RPP and its supporters were not in agreement about what the Viaduct's opportunity was. At best, RPP sent mixed messages by having its two cofounders participate in development of the 2004 PCDC plan. RPP did not counter the PCDC's framing of the Viaduct as blight, or its proposed solution (tear-down), allowing any momentum gained from the charrette to evaporate.

The project has some strong supporters, primarily from Callowhill and other adjacent neighborhoods, who often use words like stunning, rare, and serene to describe the Viaduct, "both stunning skyline vistas and a rare peaceful oasis in the heart of Center City" (Gradinger 2004). Inga Saffron of the Philadelphia Inquirer described her 2004 visit to the Viaduct where "Center City gleam[s] on the horizon like a faraway Oz. Somehow the harsh industrial landscape on its fringes makes the viaduct feel like a serene oasis, rather than a gritty outpost" (Saffron 2004). Local blogger Michael Froehlich took his cue from Saffron's 2009 article reviewing New York's High Line and argued that "demolishing the Viaduct—an estimated $35 million [to do]—would strip Philadelphia's loft district of [a] potentially valuable amenity and make it a less distinctive place to live" (Froehlich 2009).

While city officials and other supporters admit the structure is considered a blighting influence (Edelstein 2011; Urek 2011; Thompson, Radio Times 2011), they argue that it is also a really interesting elevated space (Thompson, Radio Times 2011), and a "cool space…just trying to get to the right place" (Edelstein 2011), emphasizing that the structure's height allows you "to really see the city from an entirely different perspective than you can just 30 feet below on the ground. ….. the views from up there are spectacular." (David, Radio Times 2011). Nancy Goldenberg of CCD emphasized they wanted the space to feel authentic. She also highlighted some of the amenities the space would provide, like wooden swings and seating arrangements allowing schools to use the space for an outdoor classroom (Kopp 2017).

When done in a consistent way, talking about the space's aesthetics can make a project feel closer to reality. If stakeholders are debating where to put benches, or what the plantings should look like, they have, at some level, already bought in to the project actually happening. Here, the unfinished timeline and corresponding unfinished program for the space raises questions about how successful this kind of discourse has been.

Envisioning: Access or Usability

The 0.25-mile part of the Viaduct owned by SEPTA is accessible at grade. But, how people will use the Rail Park (walking, biking, and so on) determines how users will need to access the structure above grade. Since RPP's founding, some called the Rail Park a green space, some said it could be a park, some called it a bicycle trail, some said it was a link or connector among communities, others described it as an anchor, and still others talked of it as a commuting option (Gradinger 2004; Saffron 2004). There has been a lot of disagreement about what the Rail Park would do and how it would work.

Although Section One of New York's High Line opened in 2009, this did *not* lead to consensus in terms of what the Rail Park would be; publicly, RPP was still offering differing, competing uses for the Rail Park in 2009, while disagreements were still being aired. On RPP's website, they listed "potential cross-country ski trail" in 2009, and cofounder

McEneaney "admit[ted] she has her own visions of an amenity: public space, including bike trails, walking trails or children's Park" (Brakeman 2009).

Once Paul Levy of CCD became a supporter, he began giving presentations and talks describing an esplanade-type park that would act as an anchor (Levy 2011), attempting to build buy-in. This idea of the space being primarily described as a park echoes sentiments expressed by city officials (Focht 2011; Edelstein 2011; Hoch 2011; Urek 2011). Focht, from the Parks Department, in particular, stressed the importance of understanding how the park will actually work.

There's really three phases [involved in making [it] happen]. There's raising the money. There's going through a civic engagement process to envision what this new public space would look like, you know, what do the residents and visitors want out of the space. And then ... doing the environmental remediation and building it (Focht 2011).

This approach of raising the money before fully envisioning the space is unique to Philadelphia and the Rail Park. The High Line, the 606, and the Lowline carried out and are carrying out those activities in the reverse order. March 2012 images released by Studio or Bryan Hanes Architects showed renderings of the SEPTA spur, to support moving forward with that part of the project. In all renderings, the architect, by design, showed only young people or families (Levy 2011; Romero 2017), attempting to appeal to the young demographic living in and near Center City, as well as to explicitly draw comparisons to New York's High Line, where initial renderings also focused on a younger demographic (thehighline. org). Figure 4.2 shows an from the renderings themselves, which received a very positive response from some parts of the greater Philadelphia community (Corcoran 2012; Popkin 2012; Spikol 2012; Zale 2012).

RPP and its supporters still seem torn about what the Rail Park should be—an esplanade, like New York's High Line, or something that accommodates bicycles, like Chicago's 606. Which programmatic option they choose matters for who uses the Rail Park, and how. Disagreement makes planning and coordinating more difficult. Especially when combined with contested discussions about what the park will look like, disagreement about how it will work can also make the organization seem less focused (DCnPhilly 2010; Prahalad 2011), and can decrease the likelihood that

Figure 4.2 2012 Rendering with city view

Source: philly.curbed.com

the organization is taken seriously. Most recently, CCD has moved into a central position in the project (Romero 2017), and RPP's role has been diminished. This is different from what happened in Chicago, where the Trust for Public Land was in a coordinating role, but the Friends of the 606 were constantly talked about as the entity responsible for the park in the future. While CCD has moved front and center, RPP has attempted a reset, and rebranded the park itself (Romero 2016), including a new logo, shown in Figure 4.3.

There are two trees in the logo; the larger, outer tree shape is supposed to let the viewer know this is a park. The railroad tracks are trying to represent both history (train) and project momentum. The three railroad ties

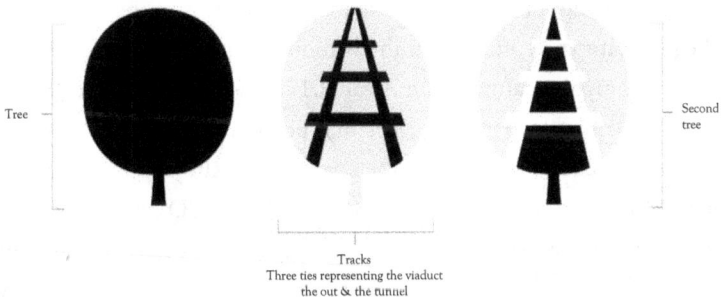

Figure 4.3 Rail Park logo components

Source: The Rail Park.

represent the three named sections of the park: the Viaduct, the Cut, and the Tunnel. The center, second tree is somewhat mysterious and invites the viewed to investigate and discover more about the park (Smith and Diction 2016). As part of the rebranding, the advocacy group's website now describes the Rail Park as "a greenway that will serve pedestrians, bicyclists, neighbors, and visitors alike…..[with] safe, beautiful pathways and gathering spaces with educational, arts, culture, health, and wellness programs" (therailpark.org). It remains to be seen if this consensus will hold.

Creating: Development and Cost

This dimension of institutional work uses discourse to highlight the capacities and skills of RPP to carry out the project. The dominant theme in this dimension was the long process of development and project cost. Like the discourse around the Lowline, and unlike the discourse in the High Line, or the 606, the secondary theme was the coalition of support-ers behind RPP. This project's discourse focused on the mostly symbolic nature of the 501c(3) group's supporters, with the exception of CCD, who has been a strong supporter for a while.

Some money has been raised for design and construction using the coalition's connections. The Rail Park's website claims "$9 million has been raised to date…from the City of Philadelphia, the Commonwealth of Pennsylvania, the Center City District, the William Penn Founda-tion, the Knight Foundation, Poor Richard's Charitable Trust, and the McLean Foundation" (therailpark.org). In 2017, the project has received some limited support from Heineken USA, which is sponsoring a small Indiegogo campaign along with the National Trust for Historic Preserva-tion. The campaign launched in April 2017 and set a 15,000 dollars goal to support completing the project's first portion, as scheduled, by 2018 (Tanenbaum 2017). The rest of the coalition of RPP supporters has not done much to bring the project closer to reality. CCD has moved into a lead role, particularly as it relates to fundraising and project coordination. That may be great for Phase 1, but the timeline for the rest of the proj-ect remains unfunded, described as an *if*, not a *when* (Kopp 2017). The project has a coalition in name, but not in action—symbols of shallow support as opposed to arranging financial resources, changing zoning requirements, or providing much beyond a list of names.

The key issues around development were and are (1) renovation versus tear-down and (2) whether the development was actually going to happen. There were large gaps in the discourse: a flurry of activity in 2004, due largely to the UPenn charrette and 2004 Chinatown Plan, then trailing off until 2007, when the High Line broke ground. There was also a shift from emphasizing development to emphasizing coalition in 2009, when the High Line's first phase opened, and the Chinatown community meeting happened.

For years, citizen groups in Chinatown have seen the demolition of the elevated Viaduct portion—which somewhat awkwardly transects their neighborhood—as the first step in developing what they call Chinatown North and other residents call Callowhill (Heller 2009; Thompson 2011; Levy 2011). John Chin, the Executive Director of the PCDC, argued that "The Viaduct has a blighting effect"; demolition "would make available a lot more land to build housing targeted for more lower-income families" (Chin, quoted in Timpane 2009). Neighborhood groups in Chinatown fear that if the Rail Park is developed, it will attract gentrification, not the mixed-income residential growth the area needs. They have a good reason to expect this. Outside groups have a history of forcing *improvements* on Chinatown, as mentioned, often dicing up and hemming in the neighborhood without benefiting it much (Thompson, Radio Times 2011). Chinatown residents are wary, as Chin was quoted as saying, of projects that are "not focused on serving the existing people in the community," that are "done in a vacuum and [do] nothing for Chinatown residents" (Chin, quoted in Timpane 2009).

It has been challenging for RPP and its supporters to discuss the opposition to their project. In describing those who wish to tear it down, RPP members and supporters use phrases like "they [Chinatown residents] want to be a victim" (Levy 2011), or "I just can't understand it, and feel like I'm never going to understand it. I wish they would come around. The[ir] argument just doesn't make sense" (McEneaney, quoted in Timpane 2009). RPP and its supporters cannot see how to assuage the feelings of the Chinatown advocacy groups who believe they took the brunt of Philadelphia's urban renewal plans or determine how to develop plans to include affordable housing in a larger plan for the area beyond initial high-level discussions.

RPP is mostly absent from fundraising discussions, even those surrounding development of the SEPTA-owned parts (Focht 2011; Levy 2012). Given the development process thus far, and the likelihood that city government will have to pay a part of the construction cost, the discourse has reflected considerable skepticism, especially post-2009. This could be related to the economic downturn, but that was only moderately mentioned in the discourse (McCabe 2011; Russ 2012; philadelphiaspeaks 2012). The links between the long development process and the nature of the neighborhood itself showed up more clearly in the discourse (Amart 2011; Levy 2012; philadelphiaspeaks 2012). There was also some contrast here with the discourse around the High Line, particularly comparing RPP and FHL in terms of the perceived skills and capacity to persevere in a contentious setting. Overall, there was more consistency in the discourse in the creating section than in the envisioning section. However, questions still remain about the abilities of RPP to realize their proposed park. CCD's involvement does not answer those questions.

Legitimating

The final part of the discourse involved connecting the project's supporting rationales to improving the neighborhood. There was a lot of discussion about New York's High Line, the only similar project in the United States currently open, and under two hours from Philadelphia. Proponents of the Rail Park referred to the High Line and its success in inspiring urban renewal as they tried to legitimate the project. However, opponents also referred to the High Line, in a negative way, to oppose the project as an elitist, gentrification initiative.

Legitimating: Neighborhood

Individual urban redevelopment projects take place in a specific part of the city; they are not just anywhere, and their location is generally not negotiable. When repurposing an existing space or structure (as distinguished from building new in a green field), the impact of the project on that neighborhood becomes even more important because the conversation is not "build it here or somewhere else," but instead "do it here or don't do it at all." That is the case for the entire length of the Rail Park (albeit with different communities); the arguments RPP and CCD were and will continue making involve how this planned park is good for the neighborhood (Kopp 2017). It is important to remember in this case that the proposed project runs through very different neighborhoods, including as extreme examples the ethnic enclave of Chinatown and the not yet gentrified, whiter Callowhill. Another set of arguments RPP and its supporters made to complement the neighborhood focus, but less successfully, was attempting to frame the issue as more than just a neighborhood issue. If RPP can change the conversation to one about the impact on Philadelphia as a city, instead of just their immediate neighborhood, they might be able to generate a wider group of supporters.

The discourse in this dimension was less fragmented than elsewhere but was contained in two irreconcilable categories. The first subtheme is about how this park could be transformative for neighborhoods, with a focus on the Callowhill neighborhood. "For the workers here, for the residents that have lived here for a long time—they don't have front stoops....or backyards...this...is a green space where they can talk to their neighbors, walk their dogs, ...and sit around after dinner and talk" (Goldenberg, quoted in Kopp 2017).

The second subtheme is primarily driven by supporters of the Chinatown or Callowhill North neighborhood, particularly Chinatown's development group (PCDC) and is about contesting the nature of Callowhill itself. The PCDC is conveying the sense that this potential park is being imposed on the neighborhood, and that the residents of Chinatown would not choose a park. The latter approach depends on understanding how Chinatown's identity has formed, listening to the argument "stop telling us what we need" (Chin 2009), and linking the Rail Park's development to developers (Spunt 2017), not community members.

Philadelphia, like other cities, has been encouraging people to move back to the downtown area (Kimmelman 2017). But, the areas that were affordable to live in, like Callowhill, lacked some key amenities, like green space. Much of the language used around transforming the Callowhill neighborhood focused on its current blighted state and its downtown location, so close to Center City—a theme used by RPP and its supporters since the group's inception. Residents of Chinatown are nervous about the changing demographics, especially in and around the elevated Viaduct portion, and they are at least partly correct that the neighborhood is changing. Figure 4.4 shows the changes in the neighborhood from the 2000 to 2010 census.

Racial composition of Philadelphia overall and rail park census tracts, 2000 and 2010

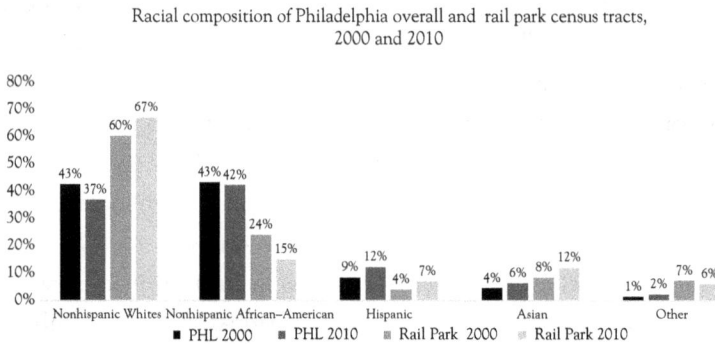

Figure 4.4 Distribution of race, Viaduct-adjacent census tracts versus greater Philadelphia, 2000 and 2010

Source: census.gov, American Community Survey Factfinder

To Rail Park supporters, a park would spur investment and revitalize an area so close to downtown that it could become the city's next neighborhood success story. It is, for Levy and his CCD organization, a Center City vision. They imagine an amenity for residents and workers. With nearly one-third of the local land still vacant, they envision a mixed-use, mixed-income neighborhood close to downtown (Center City District 2010; Levy 2011; Levy 2012; Kopp 2017). Like many American cities, Philadelphia is banking on parks and public spaces to drive social and economic progress (Kimmelman 2017). But, even in Kimmelman's recent 2017 article, focusing on work specifically done in Chicago and Philadelphia, Chicago's 606 trail and parks are given the spotlight, and the Rail Park is totally missing from the conversation. Visibility matters.

This desire to use the Rail Park as a catalyst for transformation runs right into Philadelphia's century-old Chinatown community's competing vision of survival in the face of a half dozen Center City visions that have threatened to destroy it (Timpane 2009). Chinatown residents have fought each development, often winning their battles. The Chinatown 2004 plan that called for the elevated Viaduct section to be demolished to create rectangular parcels to develop subsidized housing "gave Chinatown the sense of ownership of calling [Callowhill] Chinatown North, so this was their expansion area in their mind" (Levy 2011). Fundamental disagreement about what to call the Callowhill neighborhood matters for how united the neighborhood is or can claim itself to be.

This theme is also consistent with Philadelphia's history; William Penn's original master plan for the city assumed that its urban fabric would be regularly relieved by parks (Juday 2012). With this original goal in mind, supporters argued, the neighborhood around the elevated Viaduct is noticeably lacking in green public land (van Meter 2012). Supporters focused on how a park could be an important component in the revitalization of the area.

All of Center City…is considered rather underserved by neighborhood-accessible open space in a lot of ways and that was one of the arguments in favor of the Friends of the Rail Park, because it would bring in some acreage of open space that would be directly accessible to the people who lived within a half-mile. (Urek 2011)

Ellen Somekawa, Executive Director of Asian Americans United[2] and a RPP board member, added, "the absence of green space is a very striking thing for this neighborhood. I'd like to cut a little bit against this thing of 'are you for the poor people of Chinatown or are you for the rich people in the lofts.' What they have in common, though, is this desire for livability" (Radio Times 2011). John Hoch of the Planning Department pointed out that

---

[2] Asian Americans United's mission is to build leadership in Asian-American communities to build neighborhoods and unite against oppression. AAU has worked in Philadelphia's Asian-American communities and in broader multiracial coalitions around quality education, youth leadership, anti-Asian violence, immigrant rights, and folk arts and cultural maintenance.

our department supports the idea of [the Rail Park] as an open space element that reaches into Center City and serves the Chinatown community. . [But]—Chinatown is not the only interested party in terms of the geography where the Viaduct exists. Though they have been very successful and aggressive in claiming that territory as their own. …The notion that Chinatown is the only actor we're dealing with, here—Chinatown would love that but I don't think that's really the case. (Hoch 2011)

With development progressing slowly on the SEPTA spur, Chinatown's leadership seems cautiously open to the Rail Park idea, at least in part, and provided it includes affordable housing. Levy has laid out some ideas already, based on working with architect Cecil Baker to develop proposed housing in the existing irregular parcels; PCDC Executive Director John Chin finds them intriguing (Thompson 2011 Radio Times; Levy 2011). This kind of compromise may be what can bring the two communities together; perhaps, it will lead to a discussion or compromise about what to call the neighborhood itself. The lack of agreement on a name for the neighborhood is representative of far larger disagreements. RPP has not been able to manage the intense conflict about the phrases, images, and logics for thinking and talking about the new venture. The lack of control over the conflict has led to inertia, with the innovative process slowed while different organizational actors—PCDC, RPP, Center City, city government agencies—spar over control issues.

Legitimating: High Line

The High Line is a natural comparison to the Rail Park. The High Line is close by, it started its development process only a few years before the Rail Park, and it faced organized opposition (David 2011). Also, like the High Line, the Rail Park offers a window into a bygone industrial era and the days when cities were places where things were made and then shipped all over the country and the world. Visitors can still see the faded lettering on the sides of former industrial buildings that once served as automobile, bicycle, shoe, glass, and balloon factories (Timpane 2009; La Farge 2011).

The first High Line-related theme around the Rail Park pointed out the visitor traffic, investment spurred by development, urban development impact, and other positive attributes of the High Line. The second High Line-related theme involved explaining all the constraints Philadelphia faced in building the park and how the Rail Park was not enough like the High Line (and Philadelphia not enough like New York) to be successful.

In the first subtheme, journalists and others pointed out that like the High Line, elevated sections of the Rail Park offer stunning views of the Philadelphia skyline (Froehlich 2009; Rosof 2009; Saffron 2011; Kopp 2017), as well as intimate glimpses of everyday life in the streets below (La Farge 2011). Timpane compares the two projects in his 2009 article.

> The Highline is a disused section of elevated freight railway in Manhattan… now transformed into an elegant, elevated park. With its lush array of plants, it's eco-friendly benches and tables, it affords views of city and sky you can't get anywhere else. Philadelphia has its own candidate for a High Line Park—the Rail Park. Folks who've been up there report beautiful, singular views of the skyline and surrounding neighborhoods (Timpane 2009).

The Callowhill neighborhood in particular shares some characteristics with pre-High Line era Chelsea, one of the neighborhoods the High Line runs through. Callowhill is a blighted area of the city adjacent to established and expensive areas—even more blighted than Chelsea was. The development of the High Line put some parameters around what was actually possible to do with the Rail Park. The High Line brought in billions in private investments into the New York City and created thousands of permanent jobs. As numbers linked to the High Line's impact on surrounding neighborhoods began to circulate, supporters became even more excited.

In a Brakeman article from 2009, he quotes RPP Board Member Louis Chang as saying, "[t]he only way for that [area] to get activated is for [the Park] to get activated." He said the blocks around New York's High Line had been dilapidated but began to rebound when the park was formed. Likening that effect to the 1989 movie *Field of Dreams*, he said,

"It's like 'if you build it, they will come.' It's not even a question" (Brakeman 2009). Other media outlets and local bloggers argued that RPP's reclamation of neglected urban space (Saffron 2011) would help revitalize a community that needs green space, would create infrastructure, and would bring new development (Sundance Channel 2011) with the "same effect as the Highline did" [emphasis added] (Philly Bike Journal 2011).

On the other hand, many argue that the High Line is simply not comparable.

> [E] very few weeks I read about some new building or some new expensive addition to the landscape along the High Line or companies or developers, you know, spending millions of dollars to leverage the value they see in the High Line. I don't think that anyone expects that that would happen here, so it's a very different model. I think there's some kind of public open space amenity that could be accomplished. (Urek 2011)

Bloggers and journalists expressed concerns that "the High Line ...got built because it runs through several neighborhoods on the west side of Manhattan that had already been booming" (Philadelphiaspeaks 2012), and that it was not a case of "build it and they will come," but more like "build it and they are already there" (Rybcynski 2011). James Corner, Principal of James Corner Field Operations, a New York architecture firm that designed the High Line with Diller Scofidio + Renfro, was quoted as saying

> [d]espite the High Line's visibility and help in showing donors and residents nationwide what is possible with an abandoned trestle, ...The High Line is not easily replicable in other cities. "It's not just, 'Build a cool park and they will come.' It's, 'Build a cool park and connect it to a framework.'" (Shivory 2011)

Journalists, bloggers, and other commentators have also noted that the High Line did not revitalize its surrounding neighborhood on its own. It was the "High Line plus"—plus all the other stores and amenities that developed around the park (Heller 2009; Rybcynski 2011). Blogger

Karen Amart from PennPlanning asked an important question: "right now, …does the area attract people?" (Amart 2011). And, she expressed concerns, shared by others, that right now, some neighborhoods near the Rail Park feel uncomfortable, unsafe, and out of the way and lacks fundamental amenities (Heller 2009; Amart 2011; Sweeney 2012; PhiladelphiaSpeaks 2012). The Rail Park's elevated sections would offer amazing views of downtown, but also, in its existing state, views of incredible blight (Amart 2011).

At the same time, RPP and its supporters tried to downplay the costs of building the Rail Park relative to the High Line (Levy 2011; McEneaney 2011; van Meter 2012), explaining that they did not think that the 150 million dollars spent on Sections One and Two of the High Line (highline.org) were necessary for the Rail Park to be an asset for its neighborhoods (Loviglio 2012). They also invited FHL cofounder Josh David to talk about the Viaduct project in November 2011, where David highlighted his belief that "the Rail Park in some ways is a greater opportunity than the Highline in that it's much wider and offers you I think a lot more potential for different kinds of development as a park" (David, Radio Times 2011). Like the High Line, Rail Park supporters are trying to start small: develop one piece of the property (Levy 2012; Romero 2016; Kopp 2017) and use that to build support and encourage participation and private donations. But ,the role of the Friends of the Park group in New York was much more clearly defined than in Philadelphia, and RPP just is not as well connected as FHL, and critically, seems like they are not interested in making some important connections (Trust for Public Land, Rails to Trails Conservancy) that could help them. So, RPP—and the project—suffers by comparison.

This split in the discourse is about understanding whether or not the High Line is a good comparable, and whether or not Philadelphia can have similar, though smaller-scale success with the Rail Park as New York did with the High Line. The split, particularly given the success of the High Line, is at least in part due to the lack of fundraising to date and the lack of programming decisions. Unresolved yet, core questions about the Rail Park can interfere with the advocacy group's ability to link their project to larger conversations about urban renewal and community development.

Summary and Conclusions: What They Did Well and Not Well

Like any large-scale urban renewal project, the Rail Park faces many challenges in moving from the status quo of planning to actualization. Overcoming these challenges requires generating and maintaining momentum, creating viable coalitions of support, and a clearly articulated outcome. If the discourse around the Rail Park was supportive of this endeavor, we would consistently see individuals and organizations expressing how the project can be a solution to an existing problem, how RPP, as part of a coalition, has the ability to make the park happen, and how this project is related to other, broader, important conversations about green space, urban living, neighborhood development, and so on. That is not in the discourse.

RPP has attempted to make the case that Philadelphia needs a Rail Park, that the park makes sense for the neighborhood and city in large and small ways, and that RPP should be leading the charge for the community. To that end, they have used different images, symbols, and words to illustrate the potential benefits of the Rail Park. The discourse is tilted toward *legitimating* work—creating and supporting links to larger conversations. RPP has focused intently on gaining legitimacy for the project. Their search for legitimacy was based on a reliance (maybe even an overreliance) on Philadelphia-based groups within and parallel to city government to build legitimacy, as opposed to efforts to speak for the local community. While the discourse focused slightly more on envisioning as a secondary area, that too was heavily contested and RPP's focus came at the expense of work in the creating area.

The discourse in the envisioning dimension is heavily fragmented and contested, implying that RPP has not been successful in framing its desired solution as necessary—or even that other institutional arrangements are falling short. The creating dimension and its focus on the development process also highlight an area of challenge for RPP. The discourse around development was extremely contentious, especially related to their ability to build community support and the cost of the project. This tension spilled over into the legitimating dimension, in the area of discourse around different neighborhoods, especially Callowhill. RPP's efforts to gain project legitimacy were top-down, as opposed to the other advocacy groups studied, whose efforts were both bottom-up and top-down.

If the Rail Park is to be transformed, RPP and its supporters need to influence the dialog around it to highlight neighborhood revitalization, rather than a standalone project. RPP and its supporters have calculated economic benefits related to doing the project but developed no complete programmatic solutions. In the face of opposition and uncertainty that is not enough.

Friends of the Park groups in New York, with the High Line, and Chicago, with the 606, had a plan for each space and they consistently promoted that plan. The opposition to the High Line in New York wanted to tear down the structure, and FHL had to provide a reason to keep it. There was not deep opposition to redeveloping the 606 in Chicago, and there was also a plan to link the trail to the ground using small pocket parks. Unlike the High Line, or Lowline, the neighborhoods adjacent to the Rail Park's surrounding neighborhoods are not in a position to memorialize the history of a blighted past; that blighted past is still very much present. Urban revitalization is not about picking and choosing physical projects from other cities and sticking them into one's own, devoid of context.

The best thing that happened to RPP was CCD getting involved. But, CCD's involvement may mean that the fate of the park becomes independent of the fate of RPP. It currently appears that CCD will take control of the project, shapes the message, and provides stronger and more direct governmental direction and support because RPP cannot be an effective champion. Their ultimate role still needs clarity. Under this scenario, there will likely be a lag between the current construction of the SEPTA spur, and the Cut, the Tunnel, and the remaining part of the elevated Viaduct being developed. Reading International still controls the elevated Viaduct section, and without some real negotiations (perhaps with CCD in the mix, perhaps not) to bring it under control of whichever entity is leading the development, the project cannot be completed in the form RPP has been advocating.

CHAPTER 5

The Lowline: In the High Line's Shadow?

The proposed location of New York's Lowline is the nearly 1.5 acre former Williamsburg Bridge Trolley Terminal, just below Delancey Street, in Manhattan's Lower East Side neighborhood. The site was opened in 1908 for trolley passengers, but has been unused since 1948, when trolley service was discontinued. Figure 5.1 shows an image of the Lowline in its proposed future location.

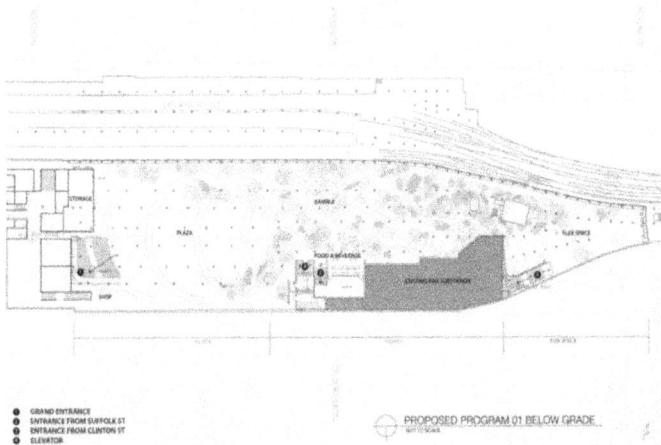

Figure 5.1 Lowline, proposed future location

Source: Reprinted from Lowline Proposal: Presented to NYC EDC, 2016.

Brief History of Civic Action

In 2009, James Ramsey and Dan Barasch discovered the underground, abandoned Williamsburg trolley terminal in the Lower East Side and developed a plan to install solar technology in the site. The project would use a series of street-level mirrors to collect and redirect the sun's rays, and then pipe it through tubes down to the space below, enabling plants and trees to grow underground. They called themselves the Delancey Underground, after the street location of the terminal. Barasch and Ramsey also set up the Underground Development Foundation, an organization under which they could organize and advocate for the project; this entity was eventually granted 501c(3) status.

By 2010, people were calling them *the Lowline* (Sweeting 2015; Yue 2017) and making connections between the High Line and Lowline. So, the two cofounders embraced the Lowline name and began using it. Unfortunately, the name change does not really connote what the cofounders were aiming for, and likely helps less than it hurts. The Delancey Underground is more descriptive, more unusual, and actually explains that people are underground.

In 2011, Ramsey and Barasch released the concept of the Lowline to the public in a highly visible New York Magazine feature, modeled after the High Line's successful use of photos in a 2001 New Yorker magazine article. Their article was accompanied by futuristic images, as shown in Figure 5.2.

Figure 5.2 The Lowline image

Source: Reprinted from Lowline Proposal: Presented to NYC EDC, 2016.

In February 2012, the team (LL) launched a Kickstarter campaign that raised over 200,000 dollars from 3,300 worldwide supporters. The Lowline used the Kickstarter money and additional funding to commission planning studies from HR&A Advisors (who also worked with the Friends of the High Line), and Arup (who worked with the Friends of the 606) to assess the viability of building a public park in the former trolley terminal. Both studies provided evidence that the idea could become a reality.

In September 2012, for a limited time, the LL installed a functioning full-scale test model of the solar technology and accompanying greenery in an abandoned warehouse directly above the actual site. The group ran another successful Kickstarter campaign in 2015 to develop and open a simulated space, which they called the Lowline lab. In October 2015, the team opened the Lowline Lab, close to the proposed future location. The lab was a free community gathering space, open to the public on weekends, that displayed the solar technology the park will use, allowed the team to experiment on growing plants underground, and hosted cultural and community events. Over 100,000 people visited the lab before it closed in March 2017.

The economic impact study HR&A Advisors completed showed the positive effect the Lowline would have on development projects being proposed for the Lower East Side's Seward Park Urban Renewal Area, or SPURA. The SPURA project affects a group of city-owned parking lots and small buildings that have stood mostly vacant or underused for 50 years. It also happens to be immediately adjacent to the planned future location of the Lowline. The Wall Street Journal in 2012 presented HR&A's findings that the Lowline would increase the value of SPURA sites by 10 to 20 million dollars and create 5 to 10 million dollars in sales, hotel, and real-estate taxes (Morgan 2012).

In 2013, the then-mayor Bloomberg and the Economic Development Corporation (EDC) unveiled plans to transform the dormant SPURA space into Essex Crossing, a 1.65 million square-foot mixed-use, multibuilding complex clustered around the intersection of Delancey and Essex Streets. Ground was broken on phase one of the project in 2015 (Sweeting 2015). Renderings show an underground retail corridor connecting the basements of the complex's three largest buildings, sitting next to the Lowline's proposed home, right below Delancey Street. A proposed above-ground site plan from 2014 shows what appear to be entrances to the Lowline immediately outside Essex Crossing Building 3. Similar plans for the Lowline's below-ground space show it sharing a southern wall with Essex Crossing's northern boundary. Integration between the two spaces is key for this to work, as the two projects are immediately next to one another, as shown in Figure 5.3.

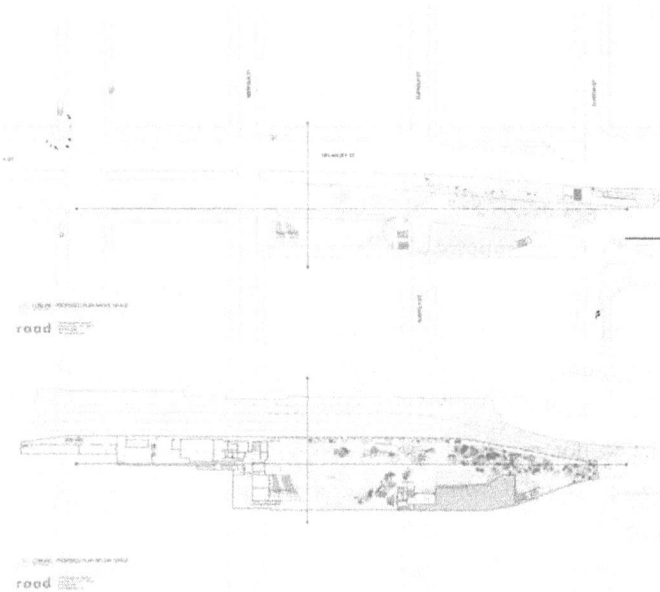

Figure 5.3 2014 Renderings of SPURA and the Lowline
Source: Reprinted from Lowline Proposal: Presented to NYC EDC, 2016.

In September 2016, the LL was granted conditional site control of the Trolley space. This designation is linked to their completing several related actions, indicating they can develop the project. First, they must hold 5 to 10 public design charrettes with the local community, along with quarterly Community Engagement Committee meetings. Second, they must raise at least 10 million dollars over the next year. Finally, they must complete schematic design documents and present them for approval by New York City's Economic Development Commission within one year. Under a best case scenario, the Lowline would open in

2021 (Mechwarrior 2016). Figure 5.4 shows an advertisement for one of the public meetings, in May 2017.

What Would You Do At the Lowline?
Free Public Workshop!

Science & Technology

Recreation

Arts & Culture

Education

Health & Wellness

WHEN   Saturday, May 6th, 10:00 AM

WHERE   Hamilton Fish Park Library
415 East Houston Street, New York, NY

WHAT   A public workshop to hear YOUR IDEAS on Lowline programming: how the space should be used. Everyone is welcome. The workshop is free and dinner will be served.

WHY   Help shape this new space in your backyard so that you can use it in the years to come.

About the Lowline: The Lowline seeks to transform an unused underground public space into a community-oriented hub, and we're continuing a community engagement process to find out what local residents want to see in this unique place. The Lowline will use innovative solar technology to bring natural light underground - providing an exciting opportunity to build a green space that's accessible year-round, and will include programming and activities.

Figure 5.4 May 2017 public meeting notice
Source: The Lo-Down.

The Lowline, while actively modeling discourse themes and community outreach on the High Line model, has been working on the project for over seven years with minimal progress. They are still attempting to develop a coalition of local community supporters, do not have money for construction, do not have a completely developed program for the space, and only recently received conditional control of the site. They have not consistently been able to change the conversation around the abandoned Williamsburg Trolley Terminal.

Discourse Themes as Mechanism for Reconciling Competing Institutional Logics

The discourse is slightly tilted toward the legitimating discourse. Although the discourse is mostly positive or neutral, the legitimating discourse also has the most negative tones overall. Table 5.1 summarizes the dominant themes within every dimension, along with a note on the tone and consistency within each theme.

Table 5.1 Summary of themes within institutional dimensions in the Lowline discourse

Dimension of institutional work	Theme	Tone of theme in discourse	Consistent use of theme in articles, interviews, discussions, and presentations
Envisioning	Access or usability	Neutral or positive	Yes
Envisioning	Aesthetic	Positive	Mostly
Creating	Development	Neutral or positive	Yes
Creating	Capacity	Neutral or positive	Mostly
Legitimating	Green	Positive	Yes
Legitimating	High Line	Neutral or positive	Mostly
Legitimating	History	Positive	Yes, especially given the historic importance of the Lower East Side
Legitimating	Neighborhood	Neutral or negative	Mixed

Envisioning

The *envisioning* discourse themes around the Lowline accounted for slightly over one-third of the discourse, and have focused on the space's aesthetics, and how the space would work. The cofounders focused on how they would "transform a forgotten piece of real estate in a city like New York and turn it into a magical public space" (thelowline.org). They have used renderings and simulated setups to demonstrate both aspects, since unlike the High Line, the 606, or the Rail Park, you cannot walk around the Lowline in its current state and get a sense of the future plan. Figure 5.5 shows a circa 2000 image of the undeveloped High Line, to provide a point of comparison.

Figure 5.5 Undeveloped High Line, pre-2000

Source: Reprinted from NYC.gov West Chelsea Zoning Proposal, 2005.

The LL says their space will provide "the unique experience of exploring dense and verdant underground gardens via winding pathways, marked by the old cobblestones and trolley tracks evoking this space's original purpose" (Barasch 2016, p. 74). The innovative solar technology needed to make this all work also gets a lot of attention in the discourse, with videos and images attempting to show how bright the proposed space will be. The envisioning imagery, as demonstrated in Figure 5.2 earlier, highlights both the plants and the solar technology.

But, while the technology is undeniably innovative, it is not enough of a hook to overcome the constraints the Lowline actually faces. The LL calls itself "the world's first underground park" (Lull and Rivera 2012, lowline.org), but in function and design appears more like a botanical garden (Lange 2016) or an atrium (Sweeting 2015). The pictures show plants in pots or planters, and no lawn equivalent to picnic upon

(Hawkins 2016; Barasch 2016). There is no view, or breeze, as Sweeting (2015) highlights, again in contrast to the High Line, as shown in Figure 5.6, the existing conditions. The simulated setup in the Lowline Lab also was very dark, as also shown in Figure 5.6.

Figure 5.6 Undeveloped Lowline space, current condition, 2016, and Lowline Lab, September 2016

Source: Reprinted from Lowline Proposal: Presented to NYC EDC, 2016, and the Author.

It is unclear how many people will see these images and think "yes, that is a park." Cofounder Ramsey even admits that "at its heart, the Lowline is a design and technology-driven project," while simultaneously calling it "the world's first underground park" (thelowline.org). The envisioning discourse has a dilemma: the themes and visuals are somewhat in conflict.

Their envisioning messaging supports the *creating* discourse in focusing on the green space they would create in the neighborhood. But, the pictures showing what the founders want to build are somewhat in conflict with the way the project is talked about. The tension between the words and pictures undercuts the strength of the *creating* discourse, as discussed next.

Creating

Creating themes focused on the development of the project and accounted for slightly less than 30 percent of the discourse. The project has many moving parts and pieces that need to be coordinated. In order for the Trolley Terminal to become a park, the Metropolitan Transportation Authority (MTA) would have to transfer control of the space to the city's EDC. The transfer has to happen because the EDC is the entity that could designate the Trolley Terminal a public space, and then place it under New York City's Parks Department control; the Parks Department would partner with the Lowline's Underground Development Foundation to build and run the park. (Sweeting 2015).

The LL has heavily mimicked the advisory structure, operational structure, and approach used by the High Line (Quirk 2015; Hawkins 2015; Surana 2015). They watched and learned as the Friends of the High Line were able to raise money, get political support, and become a parks conservancy in order to manage the park once open. Unsurprisingly, the Lowline has arranged for the High Line cofounders to sit on their board, hired similar economic and development advisors and consultants, and focused on building private philanthropy (Sweeting 2015).

New York has experience with private philanthropy, specifically dealing with urban parks, so the conservancy group model makes a lot of intuitive sense. Bryant Park, Central Park, Madison Square Park, the High Line, and Hudson River Park, among others are supported by organizations that supplement the money allocated to them by the Parks Department. The conservancies often cover more of the park's budget than the city does—75 percent of Central Park's budget, or as much as 98 percent of the High Line's budget.

In the *creating* discourse, the Lowline planners have closely tracked the High Line in their attempts to build champions for their project within city agencies. They hired the same lobbyist as the High Line (Sweeting 2015), and by 2013, had convinced several New York politicians, including both U.S. Senators, to send a letter to the EDC and the MTA encouraging them to begin discussing transferring control of the trolley terminal to the Parks Department and the Lowline organization. The letter cited the economic benefits quantified by HR&A and argued for the green space value as well (Sweeting 2015).

While the LL has taken steps to highlight the role *developing* the Lowline could play in increasing the value of real estate in the Lower East Side's neighborhood, their coalition of supporters includes hedge fund managers and neighborhood real estate developers, and that also comes through in the *creating* discourse (Hawkins 2016; Surana 2015). The LL's submission to New York's Economic Development Commission argued that they would provide the Lower East Side with "desperately needed green space" (Barasch 2016, p. 60), establish a new neighborhood hub, and be "a new venue for culture and arts... offering programming to support local youth, artists, and community organizations" (Barasch 2016, p. 63). The facility, organizers say, will be "free and open to the public five days a week, including weekends (from 6 a.m.–9 p.m. year-around)," and would (only) be closed for a "minimal number of revenue-generating events" (Barasch 2016, p. 91) like weddings or galas (McCarthy 2017). In 2017, after working with community focus groups, the LL revised this somewhat, in a presentation to the local community board. In order to keep the Lowline free and accessible for local residents, project planners are now considering a number of different steps to generate park income. Among the new options on the table are those aimed at tourists, either charging them for access to the park or asking them for donations (McCarthy 2017).

But, the team's plans for maintaining the Lowline—estimated at 2 to 4 million dollars annually (Morgan 2012; Barasch 2016)—would still depend on donations, event fees, program fees, and private money (LoDown 2016; Sweeting 2015; Barasch 2016; McCarthy 2017). Engineers who have worked on plans for the Lowline estimate that it can accommodate approximately 1,500 people, among the largest rentable event spaces on the Lower East Side. A Lowline tweet from 2015 suggests the space could host concerts, and it is not hard to imagine it becoming another Bryant Park, and hosting fashion shows or public exhibits. Figure 5.7 captures the tweet and related image.

The issue about revenues, in turn, highlights a tension between the envisioning and creating discourses: the organization is saying they are creating a community space, but is really developing the capacity to build

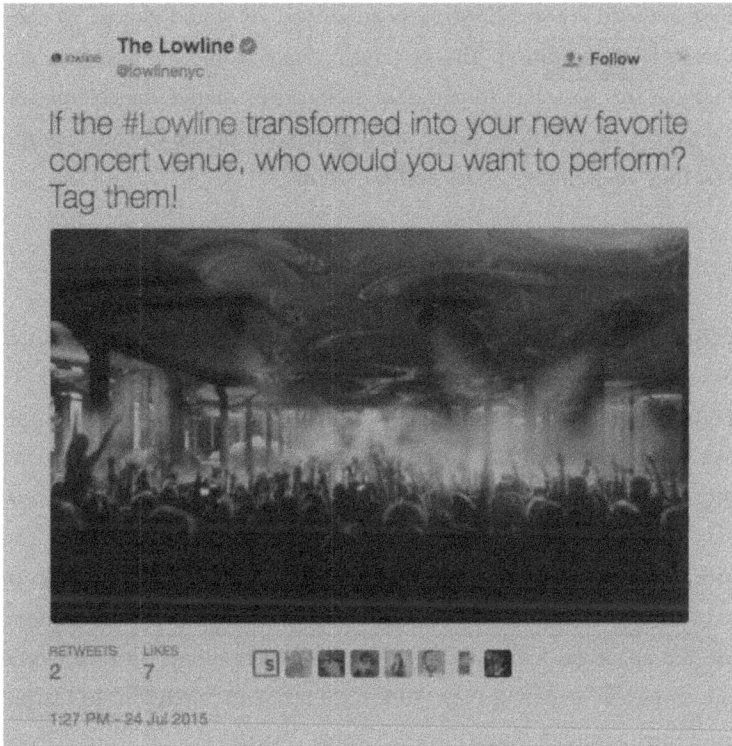

The Lowline ✓
@lowlinenyc   👤 Follow

If the #Lowline transformed into your new favorite
concert venue, who would you want to perform?
Tag them!

RETWEETS   LIKES
2   7

1:27 PM – 24 Jul 2015

Figure 5.7 Lowline tweet

Source: Twitter.

an event space, or a more extreme variation of the High Line, which is a popular tourist destination. At its core, the Lowline is a room, one that can hold up to 1,500 people (Lange 2013; Sweeting 2015). The site constraints imply that the whole space would realistically be shut down for an event, which is not what happens in a park. Shutting the entire space down from time to time reinforces the sense that this is not really a park, more like a privately funded space, or atrium, that the public gets to use.

Fundamentally, the more restricted the edges of a park—by elevation, by water, by walls —the more restricted the activities within it. High style, high maintenance, low square footage *parks* like the Lowline serve the fewest people with the most regulations (Lange 2016). In addition, New Yorkers already spend a lot of time underground using the subway system. While the High Line, the 606, or even the elevated sections of the Rail Park can feel like escapes due to elevation, it is not clear that New

Yorkers would see the Lowline as an escape, or would choose to spend more time underground. That conclusion leads to another question: who, exactly, is this park for? In this case, attempts to change the conversation to what the space will look like are undermined by the discourse around what they are going to build, and for whom.

Legitimating

Legitimating discourse themes were the strongest in the discourse, accounting for slightly less than 40 percent of the discourse overall. The major theme was the neighborhood, and how the Lowline would (or perhaps would not) benefit the neighborhood. The LL has run into challenges when they have tried to play up neighborhood-focused *legitimating* themes—developing green space, in an under-parked area of New York, working with high school students in the Lowline Lab (lowline.org), and so on. This last item matters because community members have requested that the space be focused on science and technology while providing opportunities for young New York City residents interested in learning about science and engineering (McCarthy 2017).

One of the challenges is location-specific; the Lower East Side has become an area of contention; historic buildings are being demolished as wealthy developers move into the area looking for relatively cheap real estate and a place to put new hotels, bars, and restaurants. This trend toward gentrification has landed the Lower East Side on the National Trust for Historic Preservation's list of America's Most Endangered Cities as of 2008, as the new construction "threatens to erode the fabric of the community and wipe away the collective memory of generations of immigrant families" (Chan 2008).

In response to concerns about gentrification, the LL has focused on *legitimating* discourse themes emphasizing its parallels to the High Line. As mentioned earlier, they have High Line cofounders on their board of advisors and have used the same economic and planning advisors as the High Line. Even their choice of name is meant to remind people of the High Line. But, this High Line focus has come at a cost and highlights the bundle of positives and negatives associated with the Lowline. In the Lowline *creating* discourse, as mentioned earlier, one area of focus was on the positives associated with adding green space to the Lower East Side neighborhood. Mixing *creating* and *legitimating* discourse themes, here, is challenging because linking the two means the present process of gentrification in the neighborhood receives more attention, which in turn increases tension between the two discourses.

And, most importantly, *legitimating* discourse themes attempt to change the conversation to say the Lowline is a park for the community. The Lowline's attempt to create a park from an unused remnant of below-ground transit infrastructure is a clever solution to a real and persistent problem. Community parks are a clear public good, and the Lower East Side is a neighborhood severely lacking in green space. The Lowline could create a much-needed park in a neighborhood where real estate prices on the surface make it impossible. This may be part of the founders' strategy to build support from city agencies (Hawkins 2015).

But, it is not at all clear how such a park, as it is envisioned, fits into the future of a changing Lower East Side—and whose priorities it would service. Some government officials are skeptical the Lowline will become a defining part of the city like its aerial (and named) inspiration the High Line. They wonder whether the Lowline will be a one-time attraction, primarily for tourists (Hawkins 2015; Sweeting 2015), or a magnet solely for celebrities and wealthy patrons with no stake in the community (Hu 2016).

This feeling of the existing community being left out of plans has spilled over into the discussion around the Lowline, where there are concerns about the Lower East Side's overall gentrification, especially coming from minority advocacy groups (Surana 2015; Hu 2016). The Lowline's explicit attempts to link itself to the High Line is, again, both a blessing and curse. The Lower East Side is far more populated than the High Line's neighborhood, and has an older, grittier history, one that people want to preserve.

Lowline supporters are also wrestling with definitions. The Lowline will not be a good place for barbecues, baseball games, or other activities traditionally associated with parks, nor will it be directly funded by the city (Barasch 2016); so, its status as a public space is open to debate. For a neighborhood like the Lower East Side that is extremely short on green space can feel like a cop-out to existing residents. Local community groups expressed concern about this, arguing that "[p]ublic property [should be] for the common good" (Papa, quoted in Hu 2016).

In addition, the kinds of amenities not present at the Lowline are also those that tend to appeal to communities of color (Bliss 2017), again raising questions about who the park would be for. The changing area demographics reinforce the sense that the Lowline would primarily be an engine of lifestyle-driven growth, and would not directly benefit current area residents. Figure 5.8 shows changes in area demographics from the 2000 to the 2010 census. As shown in the chart, the area around the Lowline has become more white and Asian, and less African-American and Hispanic. The city overall has become slightly less White and African-American, and slightly more Asian and Hispanic.

Racial composition of New York overall and lowline–adjacent census tracts, 2000 and 2010

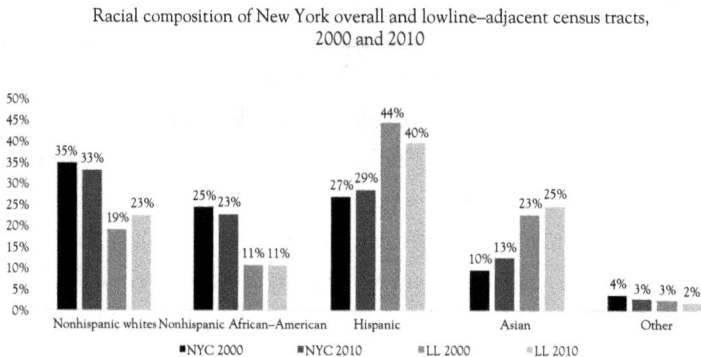

Figure 5.8 Racial composition of New York overall and Lowline-adjacent census tracts, 2000 and 2010

Source: census.gov, American Community Survey Factfinder.

Summary or What They Have Done Well and Not Well

The Lowline has its merits. The space would offer access to an otherwise unused piece of fascinating New York City history, with some incredible features, "like remnant cobblestones, crisscrossing rail tracks and vaulted ceilings" (thelowline.org). And, on a certain level, you cannot argue against adaptive reuse of unused space. The technology is fascinating, too—and potentially transformative. There are several other spaces like the abandoned Trolley terminal throughout New York City, and if this technology works, the potential to use it elsewhere is huge.

The Lowline has put forth striking designs, but they face the problem of internal inconsistency. In both the success stories New York's High Line and Chicago's 606 the advocacy group could find a theme, or several, that linked the messages targeted at each of the constituencies with pots of money available for the project. The Lowline has not found that theme or set of themes. The largest pot of money is probably from public agencies and depends on the park being a park. But, as highlighted earlier, it is not really a park. Hence, the problem.

To paraphrase Lewis Carroll's *Alice in Wonderland*, they need to say what they mean and mean what they say. If team LL straightforwardly describes what they are really planning, their project feeds community fears about gentrification, and creates an opportunity for opposition to coalesce against it. Many members of the community are not happy about rich developers trying to build what looks like a fancy plant museum, in an underground room, in the middle of their gritty, historic neighborhood (Hawkins 2015; Hu 2016). If team LL does not straightforwardly describe what they are really planning, in order to make themselves most likely to get public money, the renderings and space descriptions are in conflict with each other, and with the real constraints of the space. The founders seem to acknowledge the bind they placed themselves in, and have begun calling the space a "culture park" (Lange 2013) because it is not open to the sky. So, now the space is a *park*, not a park? That confuses people more, not less. It appears the Lowline founders have made a devil's bargain in their choice of descriptive adjectives.

For abandoned sites to be transformed, for the conversation around them to change to support those transformations, requires advocacy groups, "with their ongoing...and embedded activities, ...[to] provide [literal and metaphorical] spaces in which meaning is generated, making explanations possible from which we can build...expectations" (Fine, quoted in Sassatelli 2010, p. 91). As the groups provide the space to generate meaning, they also, hopefully, provide the space to use the meanings generated to change the conversation around their projects. Thus far, the meanings generated around the Lowline remain unclear.

CHAPTER 6

Cross-Case Comparisons and Conclusions

Each of the Friends of the Park groups is an institutional entrepreneur, trying to accumulate enough resources to turn abandoned industrial spaces into urban park space, creating a new kind of institution. The ways in which the proposed park embodies a certain, semi-private conception of a public amenity and draws aesthetic inspiration and money from governments, philanthropists, and local community members is central to the story told here. The Friends of the Park groups need to communicate and reconcile a variety of themes to make the specific abandoned structures into parks. Understanding where each project is helps situate analyses. For these four cases, three related outcomes can be considered measures of success, and Table 6.1 summarizes each case's outcome measures.

Common threads in all projects are the involvement of local community 501(c)3 groups, forming organizations, raising capital, and cultivating the support of local government agencies. These institutional entrepreneurs are trying to develop innovative, nontraditional, and incredibly complex projects, requiring multiple coalition partners. To be successful, they must reconcile an institutional logic of urban park development with a logic of profit-driven economic interest. Under certain conditions, explained in the case studies, discourse themes can be a powerful reconciliation mechanism for competing institutional logics. Instead of being driven from the top-down, the successful 501c(3) groups are combining elements of multiple strategies with a sense of place.

There was a concerted effort in both New York's High Line and Chicago's 606 to gather community input and ensure the design responded to the wishes of the communities that live, work, and play around the spaces. This has been particularly beneficial in Chicago, where the four neighborhoods the 606 runs through vary in terms of

Table 6.1 Case outcomes

Outcome	New York, High Line	Chicago, Bloomingdale Trail	Philadelphia, Rail Park	New York, Lowline
Groundbreaking and construction of these parks	• Section 1 opened in 2009 • Section 2 opened in 2011 • Section 3 opened in 2014	• Phase 1 opened in 2015 • Raising money for Phase 2, from public and private sources • Very preliminary discussions about Phase 3 extending the 606 east from its existing terminus at Ashland Avenue to below the Kennedy Expressway and over the river via an 1899 swing bridge once used for freight train service	• Construction for SEPTA spur in process, estimated to open in 2018 • Some funding in place for SEPTA spur construction, but still needs to raise money to complete construction • No complete timeline for the overall project	• Opening estimated 2021
The use of the park, once open	• Most recent annual count seven million (high line.org)	• 1.6 million in first 12 months • Estimated 1.84 million users in 2017 • Estimated 2,275 bicycle trips daily , or 750,000–825,000 annual bike trips	• Pre-opening estimates: 175,000 neighborhood residents in surrounding areas • 20 percent growth in residents over the last 20 years • High-density mixed use area: 280,000 workers	• 100,000 visitors to the Lowline Lab in under two years • Current estimates at least 200,000 Lower East Siders in the immediate neighborhood
Who uses the park	• 25 percent local • 25 percent other NY • 50 percent tourists	• No numbers available below totals • Programming implies focus on immediate area	No numbers available	No numbers available

ethnicity and socioeconomic status. Like the 606, Philadelphia's Rail Park runs through very different neighborhoods, varied in ethnicity and socioeconomic status, some of which are gentrifying and some of which are not. Yet, the Friends of the Rail Park in Philadelphia have not managed to get sustained community input into the process in a way that affects proposed designs, gets buy-in, or gives the project momentum. CCD's involvement seems to be changing that somewhat, with the group making efforts to include the community in Phase 1. To date, the RPP has been unsuccessful in developing, using, and reconciling themes describing who they are, as an entity speaking for the community, or the social justice implications of bringing green space to an underserved area, even as the CCD has pushed construction. Other themes have been developed and used in ways that are hard to understand and are often irreconcilable.

Community support matters for the success of these projects; people who participate in the development process are more likely to feel invested in the resulting public spaces (pps.org). Over time, the Friends of the Park groups have to do outreach with the adjacent community or communities, take time to understand the complexities of the communities, learn why the communities feel special or unique, and ensure that the discourse around the proposed spaces acknowledges those particularities. Each group's efforts to design and advocate for each park rely on both place-specific themes and more global themes in the discourse. Comparing these cases, there are three ways these entrepreneurs attempt to reconcile competing institutional logics, and change the conversations around these abandoned industrial spaces, summarized in Table 6.2.

Enhancing Approach to Reconciling Logics

In the successful cases of New York's High Line and Chicago's 606, envisioning and creating discourse themes enhanced and strengthened each other, as did creating and legitimating discourse themes. In New York's High Line, the aesthetics theme dominated in the High Line's envisioning dimension, at least partially because of the arts-related backgrounds of many of the advocacy group's members. Robert Hammond emphasized that, from the beginning, there was a commitment to design. "It wasn't

Table 6.2 *Strategies for reconciling competing logics*

Strategy for reconciling competing logics	New York's High Line	Chicago's 606	Philadelphia's Rail Park	New York's Lowline
Enhance (or not)	• Envisioning and creating discourses enhancing each other • Creating and legitimating discourses enhancing each other	• Envisioning and creating discourses enhancing each other • Creating and legitimating discourses enhancing each other	• Envisioning and creating discourses weakening each other • Creating and legitimating discourses weakening each other	• Envisioning and creating discourses weakening each other • Creating and legitimating discourses weakening each other
Connect (or not)	• Aesthetics and neighborhood themes connecting • Discourse balanced and consistent across themes and dimensions	• Access or usability and neighborhood themes connecting • Discourse balanced and consistent across themes and dimensions	• Creating and neighborhood, history themes connecting—includes mention of gentrification • Discourse not balanced or consistent across themes and dimensions	• Creating and neighborhood themes connecting includes mention of gentrification • Discourse somewhat balanced and consistent across themes and dimensions
Flex (or not)	• Legitimating neighborhood themes responding over time as the neighborhood changes includes mention of gentrification	• Differences in neighborhoods acknowledged includes mention of gentrification	• Creating themes responding over time to changes in the neighborhood • Legitimating Neighborhood themes responding over time includes mention of gentrification	• Aesthetics theme and creating themes causing each to change slightly to stay consistent • Legitimating neighborhood themes responding to changes over time includes mention of gentrification

enough for us to save this and put up a planter. All along there…we were going to make a commitment to design" (Behance Team 2009).

As part of their appeal to the aesthetic, in New York, Friends of the High Line (FHL) consistently focused on the 1.5 miles of open space available. Manhattan is so congested, and any amount of open space is so rarely available, that prominent supporters like von Furstenberg and Diller were intrigued by the possibilities (Hammond 2011). In the case of New York, FHL's cofounders clearly had a bold vision (Ciabotti 2011; Stone 2012) and actively promoted pictures and renderings very early on (Gopnik 2001; Hammond and David 2007; Behance Team 2009; Hammond 2011; Diane von Furstenberg 2011). FHL's ability to frame the discourse around open space was directly linked to and supportive of their coalition of supporters, financial and otherwise. In this case, the group connected with the target audiences, and the design clearly communicates the intended change—critical for a project so complex (Prahalad 2011).

FHL got financial donations and expressions of support from individuals and groups not normally involved in public works projects, as described in detail in Chapter 2. FHL creating discourse highlighted how the group created new coalitions of interested parties coming together to work on the project. This unusual coalition, and the sheer amount of money FHL raised, highlighted the group's skill at convincing government officials, supporters, and other interested parties that they could turn the High Line into a park.

Friends of the 606 in Chicago consistently focused on how the space would be used, which was partly based on their source of funding commitments. Knowing that the project would be funded primarily through the Federal Congestion Mitigation Air Quality (CMAQ) program, and thus was required to have a significant bicycle component, brought this theme to the forefront. Unlike the High Line in New York, and due to the need to accommodate bicycles, the Bloomingdale Trail is accessed via parks and ramps. Focusing on the 606's access parks and connections between the ground and the Trail has some spillover between envisioning and creating discourse for the FBT. It was able to show community members that the access parks could open even before the Trail did, which made the whole project seem more imminent than it was. This increased community confidence that FBT could actually get the project to happen.

The creating discourse also emphasized FBT's ability to get the project opened at minimal direct taxpayer cost, as described in Chapter 3, and it allowed FBT to use how the 606 needs to be accessed as the anchoring point for their envisioning discourse. While FHL's creating discourse and corresponding crossover into envisioning focused on their capacity to get city residents to donate and become supporters, the connections between the two dimensions in Chicago focused on FBT's capacity to separate the two sources of support required to open the park—the financial and the community participation. Their organizational capacity was linked to buffering Chicago city residents from the project's financial demands. This discourse has changed slightly over time, as FBT has needed to raise money for Phase 2, and that fundraising pressure has led to partial park closures for events paying rental fees (Hauser 2017; Hertzberg 2017).

The two less successful groups were not able to use discourse themes in different dimensions to enhance or strengthen each. In the envisioning discourse, RPP tried to focus on what the park could look like, in contrast to the surrounding blight, and called it open space or green space, without clearly explaining what it would actually be. As mentioned in Chapter 4, unlike the High Line, the 10 neighborhoods adjacent to the Rail Park are not in a position to memorialize the history of a blighted past. They are also not particularly interested in doing so, as the blight is still present for some of them. When RPP and its supporters tried to appeal to aesthetics in the discourse, and talked about how beautiful the elevated Viaduct section could be, the resulting discourse became dominated by opposition that highlighted the extent of the current blight instead of focusing on the Rail Park as a possible solution.

RPP and its supporters were unable to frame creating themes in a way that capitalized on the possibilities, assuaged anxieties, or even took advantage of momentum created by the envisioning discourse. While students at Philadelphia-area universities worked in intensive week-long charrettes many times over the last 10 years, RPP did not effectively publicize those efforts, capitalize on the output from those events, or expand on them. The charrettes had passing write-ups in newspapers (Saffron 2004), but generally came to be seen as *pretty pictures* (McEneaney 2011) instead of as a starting point for discussion of real opportunities; this framing appeared in the creating discourse as questions and skepticism about whether RPP could put together a coalition of support to make the Viaduct a reality. When CCD in effect took over the project, it did not reduce the skepticism around RPP. The consequences of sidelining RPP are still not clear.

LL has run into challenges when they have tried to use legitimating and creating themes in conjunction. The Lower East Side has become an area of contention; historic buildings are being demolished as wealthy developers move into the area looking for relatively cheap real estate and a place to put new hotels, bars, and restaurants. This gentrification has landed the Lower East Side on the National Trust for Historic Preservation's list of America's Most Endangered Cities as of 2008, as the new construction "threatens to erode the fabric of the community and wipe away the collective memory of generations of immigrant families" (Chan 2008). While the neighborhood needs more green space, community residents are nervous about the changes that have come, and those projected to come.

In response to concerns about gentrification, LL has focused on the creating discourse themes emphasizing its organizational parallels to the High Line, and on the positive legitimating discourse themes associated with developing green space, in an under-parked area of New York, and so on. As mentioned earlier, they have High Line cofounders on their board of advisors and have used the same economic and planning advisors as the High Line. Even their choice of name is meant to remind people of the High Line.

But focusing on the High Line to such an extent leads to a sense that the Lowline people might not be able to develop an overall benefit to the existing community, as the focus is then not on the Lowline's immediate community or what they need. In the creating discourse, the Lowline planners highlight the role that *developing* the Lowline could play in increasing the value of Lower East Side real estate. Focusing on the potential economic benefits of the Lowline is an attempt to mix creating and legitimating discourse themes. The challenge in doing this is that the present process of gentrification in the neighborhood receives more attention, which in turn increases tension between the two discourses.

And, most importantly, legitimating discourse themes attempt to change the conversation to say the Lowline is a park for the community. This may be part of the founders' strategy to build fiscal support from city agencies (Hawkins 2015). However, some government officials wonder whether the Lowline will be a tourist attraction (Hawkins 2015), or a magnet for celebrities and wealthy patrons (Hu 2016). The skepticism expressed by government officials reinforces the weakness exposed in the creating discourse—just what are LL backers supporting, and for who? Is it a park? Is it an elite space community members get to use? Is it somewhere to display very cool solar technology? That weakness in turn undermines the attempts to drive a park development narrative in the legitimating discourse.

Connect Approach to Reconciling Logics: Balance and Consistency

The distribution of discourse along the three dimensions of institutional work, and the consistency of message within each dimensions, reflects the advocacy group's ability to develop coalitions of support behind the project. Balance matters, to a point; even getting the design part perfect is not enough to make a project successful. Critically, focusing on the design (envisioning) without straightforward and coherent details of how a project will get there (creating) and how the neighborhood will look when it is complete (legitimating) just does not work; "if it's completely open and not clear how you would actually do it, the imagination is just not there" (Prahalad 2011).

In the FHL case in New York, the discourse showed the capacity of the FHL to envision, create, and legitimate the High Line, with creating and legitimating dimensions dominating the presence of envisioning themes in the discourse. As described in Chapter 2, as the neighborhood around New York's High Line became more gentrified, there was a corresponding increase in negative tones in the legitimating dimension about the impact on the neighborhood. The mixed discourse around the High Line Park reflects neighborhood dissatisfaction, but because the park is already open, there is no power to change anything.

The discourse around the 606 showed a focus on legitimating and envisioning. In addition, both the Chicago's 606 and post-opening

High Line discourses were close to equally balanced across the three ECL dimensions, indicating they were communicating at all levels; the main difference was the emphasis placed on the creating discourse. The Chicago's FBT discourse generally reflected a more consistent treatment of the dominant themes than the later New York's FHL discourse.

Like the 606, the Rail Park and Lowline discourses favored legitimating and envisioning discourse at the expense of the creating discourse. But, unlike the 606 discourse, this split has been less successful. The Friends of the Rail Park discourse has shown a contested capacity to envision, limited ability to create, and mixed legitimation. Themes within the envisioning dimension kept focusing on trying to explain, repeatedly and often contradictorily, all the options for what the park could be instead of making sure images were relatable to the community.

Relatability is important; something can look great and not be relatable and thus not garner support (Prahalad 2011). The themes in the discourse around the Rail Park did not interact with the sociology of Philadelphia as a city, and this may partially explain RPP's struggles to connect with the surrounding communities. The themes in the legitimating dimension were focused on arguing with the opposition about whether the project was good for the neighborhood instead of trying to develop advocates within the Chinatown community. Again, CCD coming in and trying to connect may be a short-term fix, or more than that; it is still too early and uncertain to tell. Figure 6.1 shows the distribution of discourse dimensions for all the projects.

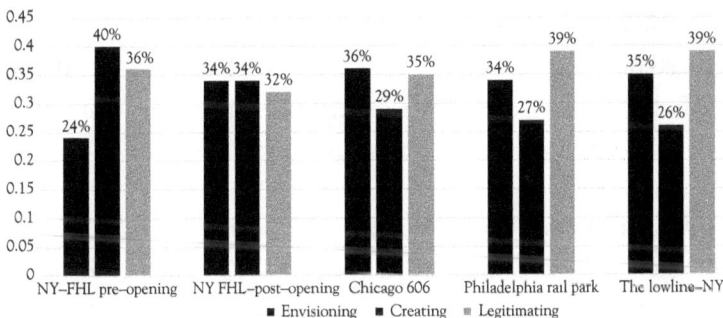

Figure 6.1 *Comparative distribution of institutional work in the discourse*

Before opening High Line Section One, the dominant dimension was the creating discourse, the capacity of FHL to carry out the project. The legitimating discourse followed closely behind, with its focus on links to larger conversations about the Chelsea and Meatpacking District neighborhoods. This was true both overall and over time, as described in detail in Chapter 2. While the discourse around the High Line before it opened was not equally balanced, the dominance of the creating discourse provided details linked to how and when the park's first section would open, and how it would be funded; it was a very specific discourse. In addition, the High Line project opened in stages, requiring repeated progression from idea to execution. FHL combined a focus on its own organizational capacity and extensive financial backing with focus on how the High Line would enhance and benefit the neighborhood. This push was pragmatic and effective, resulting in the public having a broader view of the project.

In the case of the Friends of the Rail Park in Philadelphia, the group relied on top-down legitimacy due to relationships with government officials and foundations, and this was not combined with bottom-up legitimacy based on the backing of the neighborhood. This top-down focus led to two negative outcomes for RPP. First, their focus continued to be on legitimacy invoked by claiming support from city officials—hoping that somehow this would lead to the project being taken more seriously, or their efforts to move the project forward would gain momentum. Their efforts to claim *endorsement from below* from the community continued to fall short, and in the discourse it appeared that RPP gave up, somewhat, on attempts to win over Chinatown. Second, RPP continued to focus on the legitimating discourse to shore up their case. But, a fragmented and contested discourse in the legitimating dimension is problematic, because it means the organization is not being accepted by its environment (Kostova and Zaheer 1999). This has the effect of making the project seem smaller, not larger, particularly combined with the decreased importance in the discourse of the organization's capacity.

For LL, there was a lot of time spent developing and using the legitimating dimension themes about how the project was good for the neighborhood, and attempting to connect back to the neighborhood's deep and rich history. There was also a lot of attention paid to the space's technology in the envisioning discourse—how it would work, how bright the space could be, and so on. The lack of time in the creating discourse could also indicate a lack of sureness about just what was being created.

LL has some of the same issues as RPP. Like RPP, the Lowline project has relied more on top-down legitimacy due to relationships with government officials, High Line cofounders, and High Line advisors, and less on bottom-up legitimacy based on the backing of the neighborhood. Claiming support from city officials helps to a point, the group was awarded site control in 2016, but with a list of conditions for the group that have yet to be met. It is still unclear how successful efforts to claim endorsement from the surrounding community will be.

In Figure 6.1, both the 606 discourse and that of the High Line post-opening show a nearly balanced split among the three dimensions of venture viability. This split, combined with the *consistency* found in the dominant themes, could show the coalition building and maintenance in both cases. Each type of institutional work happens at a different level; so, understanding how to influence the discourse at each level could well be a determinant of organizational capacity and growth for the advocacy group in each case.

The FHL approach to the discourse around the High Line is also consistent with Jane Jacobs' analysis of types of parks: when Jacobs talks about parks, she breaks them down into community parks, like Washington Square in New York or Rittenhouse Square in Philadelphia, and destination parks such as Central Park in New York (Jacobs 1961). These are two different classes of parks, and it is unfair to treat them the same way.

Essentially, destination park amenities need to attract people from all over the city, while neighborhood parks need to directly serve their neighborhoods. Lots of parks fail, Jacobs argues in *The Death and Life of Great American Cities*, because they either (a) attempt to be a destination park without destination park-type amenities or (b) attempt to be a neighborhood park without offering good neighborhood service. Analyzing FHL's discourse around the High Line using this approach, the envisioning themes began to change to emphasize the destination amenities provided by the High Line (Benepe 2012; Stone 2012). The 606's envisioning discourse also focused on neighborhood amenities.

Both the Rail Park and LL seemed caught between the two different kinds of parks Jacobs described, and the envisioning discourse was unclear whether the parks were supposed to be neighborhood parks or destination parks.

A neighborhood park fails because it fails to directly interact with the sociology of the city (Jacobs 1961). When a group can get consensus on what the park should be, or how it might work, those points of consensus become connection points upon which to build more consensus, and the group is able to link the points of consensus together. As in the case of the Friends of the Rail Park or, to some extent, the Lowline, when there is no consensus, where there are contested themes, the group spends much of its time and effort trying to build consensus, not trying to build on existing consensus.

The successful groups had consistent, un-fragmented, at least neutral, and mostly uncontested discourse in all three dimensions. While the Friends of the 606, the Friends of the Rail Park, and the Lowline had less than one-third of the discourse focusing on themes in the creating dimension, they did so for different reasons. Table 6.3 summarizes the important discourse themes in each case by type of institutional work proposed by Tracey, Phillips, and Jarvis (2011).

In the case of the FBT, Chicago, I believe they spent less time on creating because there was funding available for the trail to be completed at a certain level of finish, and they had a high level of mayoral support in a city with a traditionally strong mayor's office (see Chapter 3 for more detail). In other words, they did not focus as much on that dimension because they did not need to. By contrast, RPP did not focus on creating because they could never get past the disagreements about what the elevated Viaduct section was or if anything should be done, and their support at the government level was shallow, and mostly a show. And, LL did not focus on creating because they spent most of their time on two things: first, discussing what the space would look like underground and how the technology would keep it from feeling dark (for obvious reasons), and second, trying to connect to larger conversations about the neighborhood and this space as a neighborhood amenity.

Table 6.3 *Important institutional work themes, by case*

Dimension	New York's High Line pre-opening	New York's High Line post-opening	Chicago's 606	Philadelphia's Rail Park	New York's Lowline
Envisioning	Aesthetics	Aesthetics	Access or usability	Aesthetics access or usability	Aesthetics or design
Consistent treatment of theme within dimension	Yes, consistently positive	Yes, consistently positive	Yes, neutral in tone	No, opponents framing Viaduct as blight and supporters describing the opportunity were equally strong in the discourse	Mostly, the solar technology dominates the talk of design
Creating	FHL capacity	Development and cost	FBT capacity	Development and cost	Development and cost
Consistent treatment of theme within dimension	Yes, consistently neutral and positive	Slightly mixed between framing of cost versus investment in project	Yes, consistently neutral and positive	Mixed between neutral and negative—framed as cost and many open questions about who would or how to pay for the project	Slightly mixed between framing of cost versus investment in project
Legitimating	Neighborhood	Neighborhood	Neighborhood High Line	Neighborhood High Line	Neighborhood High Line
Consistent treatment of theme within dimension	Mixed positive discussion	More mixed more negative tones in the discussion	Yes, mostly neutral and positive	No, opponents and supporters do not agree on what to call the neighborhood or whether to frame the Viaduct as another High Line or not	Very mixed—positive tones about benefits are matched by negative gentrification tones in the discussion

Flex Approach to Reconciling Logics: Acknowledging and Responding to the Physical and Demographic Realities of the Sites Surrounding the Proposed Parks

In all cases, long-time neighborhood residents complaining about changes in the neighborhoods adjacent to the proposed parks are correct: their neighborhoods are changing. Since the last census, all three areas have become whiter and more affluent. In the areas around the (proposed) parks, which are close to downtown and ripe for development, these changes have been stronger and more pronounced than city-wide changes over that same time period. Figure 6.2 illustrates the increase in population percentage of non-Hispanic Whites in each of the cases since the last census, and city-wide changes in population percentage for non-Hispanic Whites over that same time period.

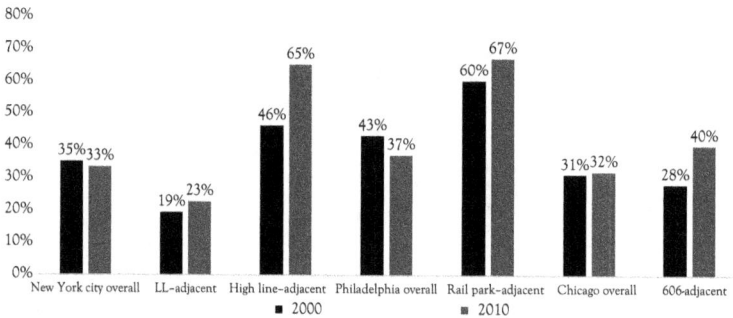

Figure 6.2 Change in non-Hispanic White population, New York, Philadelphia, Chicago, and park-adjacent census tracts, 2000 and 2010

Source: census.gov, American Community Survey Factfinder.

Figure 6.3 illustrates the substantial increases in median household income in the park-adjacent census tracts as compared with city-wide changes between the 2000 and 2010 censuses.

As discussed in Chapters 2 and 5, the High Line is surrounded by new luxury residential buildings, low-income housing projects, and everything in between, and the Lowline neighborhood is about to see its own real estate explosion. It is a familiar story, New York's mixture of rich and poor, especially in Manhattan. In Chelsea, in particular, the influx

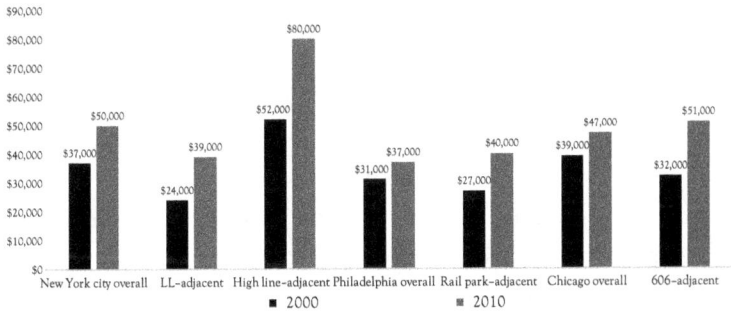

Figure 6.3 Median household income, New York, Philadelphia, Chicago, and park-adjacent census tracts, 2000 and 2010 (rounded to the nearest thousand)

Source: census.gov, American Community Survey Factfinder.

of wealthy people has pushed up real estate values dramatically in High Line-adjacent neighborhoods since 2003 (McGeehan 2011). This is a benefit to those who already own (because their apartments increase in value) and a challenge to anyone who wants to buy or rent. Commercial rents have also increased, resulting in pushing out small neighborhood services and stores and replacing them with upscale boutiques and restaurants (Feeney 2011; Humm 2012).

In Chicago, like New York, there was anxiety in the legitimating discourse about the effects of gentrification. The 606 runs through four very different neighborhoods, increasing in affluence as you move west to east. The concerns about gentrification come from the western, more Hispanic neighborhoods, and even rail trail conversion advocates admit that gentrification has happened in other urban areas once rail trails are converted to recreational use (Oberg 2011). The 606's designers made programming choices implying this park is primarily for the neighborhood's residents, however, and that somewhat assuages residents' anxieties. The designers arrived at these programming choices partly by considering the space's physical constraints and partly through multiple community visioning meetings. The multiuse path is designed to be a commuting option for those biking to work, walking to work, or as a walk-to-school option for children attending one of the dozen schools near the path.

The access points are primarily neighborhood pocket parks. Opening the access point parks first enabled FBT to publicize project momentum, allowed the project to get some sense of park usage, and encouraged community participation. There are also benefits to the community, identified as one of the most park-poor areas of the city, due to the focus on improving the neighborhood by adding these parks. The discourse around the pocket parks, in particular, focused on the lack of green space in the neighborhood, and this focus reinforced the sense that the project is good for the neighborhood. As Lucy Gomez-Feliciano of LSNA pointed out,

> we were looking for something that would allow residents to be more active—to have more places to exercise—and the trail and parks do that. But it's not like Englewood or the West Side here. There are no vast parcels of available land. This was a genius idea. We need green space. These are dense communities (Gomez-Feliciano 2011).

By contrast, to date, as reflected in the discourse around the Rail Park, RPP has not coherently engaged the residents of the neighborhoods of Callowhill or Chinatown, two of the neighborhoods along the proposed park's elevate the Viaduct section. In fact, attempts to create a neighborhood improvement district in Callowhill failed, despite City Council support—one of the few times, if not the only time, that has happened (Brey 2012). Inconsistent interactions with the community are surprising because the RPP members primarily came out of the local neighborhood association (CNA.org); in theory, they have some familiarity with the Callowhill area. The lack of connection with Chinatown residents was evident since the 2004 Chinatown North plan and subsequent meetings. At the most basic level, RPP appears unable to connect with the surrounding neighborhoods, to develop evangelists and advocates in all parts of the surrounding communities. This failure is significant because it gives credence to the counter-trope Chinatown PCDC's leaders have been pushing since 2006, arguing "no grassroots support for a landscaped esplanade truly exists in either the Callowhill loft district or Chinatown sections" (Dougherty 2006). CCD's involvement may give RPP time to shore up these weaknesses, or may just paper over them.

Throughout the discussion around the Rail Park, there are also concerns about the area's perceived overall gentrification, especially coming from the vocal Chinatown advocacy groups. One of the issues facing the development is the combination of sparse local population and the perceived lack of a wide-ranging draw in the neighborhood, not likely to encourage new residents. As discussed in Chapter 4, there is also currently little in some of the neighborhoods that could pull in day-trippers or tourists (Amart 2011), and the project is just far enough off of the beaten path to not have enough gravity on its own. So, the project has the double hurdle of there not being enough in the neighborhood to attract more people to live there, and not enough in or near the neighborhood to encourage spillover tourism.

What makes the Philadelphia case different from the discussions around the High Line, the Lowline, or Chicago is that the proposed amenity is seen as a catalyst for kick-starting revitalization instead of being a result of it. If, a decade ago, the neighborhoods near the Rail Park's elevated sections took off the way other surrounding Philadelphia neighborhoods have, this would be a moot point—the project, very likely, would have been completed a few years ago. RPP wants to link the development of the park to development of the neighborhood and to Philadelphia's history. But, it does not acknowledge the views of the ethnic enclave Chinatown, or that Chinatown's expansion plans for Callowhill include calling it "Chinatown North" (Heller 2009). The lack of acknowledgement of the demographic reality at least partly explains the lack of community support for RPP and its plans, notwithstanding Center City District's (CCD's) community efforts.

In the case of the Lowline, the project would offer access to an otherwise unused and unavailable piece of forgotten and fascinating New York City history. Adaptive reuse of unused urban space makes intuitive sense. There is also an impressive technological appeal. From a design perspective, the solar irrigation technology seems both innovative and necessary. So, while it is hard to deny the initial appeal of the Lowline's futuristic concept, the draw it would have as a repeat destination for Lower East Side residents, once they have visited once and satisfied their curiosity, is unclear.

Of far larger impact on the neighborhood is the connection between the project and the Seward Park Urban Renewal Area (SPURA) Essex Crossing project, which began construction in 2015 (Sweeting 2015).

That project will bring further change to the look and feel of the already-gentrified surrounding neighborhood, and clash with what is left of the Lower East Side's history as a working-class pocket in Lower Manhattan. And, the project's scope, alone, will bring commuters, tourists, businesses, and new residents to the area. At the center of all this change could be the Lowline.

The Lowline has chosen to highlight the role it could play in increasing the value of the surrounding real estate as SPURA and other projects come to fruition. That message is not designed for current residents. Yes, the Lowline is being supported by people with financial and ideological interests in the continued growth of New York's real estate values—the island of Manhattan is only so large, and SPURA is a massive opportunity for development. It is also true that supporting the Lowline can be framed as creating *green space* without sacrificing any of the incredibly valuable surface-level square footage—a huge added benefit.

When push comes to shove, a public space created mostly from private money has to favor the needs and preferences of those funding it. This phenomenon played out in the High Line development since the beginning, with the named sections of the park, and is beginning to play out in Chicago as well (Hauser 2017; Hertzberg 2017). Most of the millions needed to build the Lowline are projected to come from private philanthropy. SPURA's commitment to solidifying the Lower East Side as a tourist destination suggests a space that seems set up for single visits—either tourists or the curiosity of residents checking out the space or attending a one-off event. The Lowline, thus, seems designed to function more as a tourist benefit than as a setting for residents' spontaneous leisure or local activity.

The Lowline's link to the Essex Crossing complex, and its need for philanthropic largess, event and programming fees, open the door to a decreased commitment to public access, a type of semi-privatization with a long history among New York's parks. Condominiums at Essex Crossing are already listed at over 1 million dollars (essexcrossing.com). It seems the Lowline is being designed, funded, and developed to satisfy the priorities of a specific class of residents, developers, and politicians— those who measure a project's success by economic and financial metrics, instead of in terms of its use as a park or a community space.

Concluding Thoughts

As American downtowns repopulate and increase their density, green space becomes more of a premium. Very few open lots that could be turned into parks remain around urban cores; often, the land that becomes available is linked to the industrial, forgotten past. At the same time, city governments rarely have room in their budgets to redevelop the abandoned industrial spaces, so, they need private funders to bankroll these projects, at least in part.

But there is another piece, affecting those left behind. Abandoned infrastructure generally has park-poor, low-income communities of color living near them. Planners and designers, who are usually elite and White, may try to engage residents in dialog; they often meet with mixed success, or even fail (Bliss 2017).

Here is a dilemma that the cities face: improving pieces of abandoned infrastructure makes the cities more attractive and nicer places to live. That should be a goal of every city. But, once a city becomes a more attractive place to live, gentrifying starts, the laws of supply and demand kick in, and rents and housing prices go up (Budds 2016; Quintana 2016; Institute for Housing Studies 2017; Jacobs 2017). Turning abandoned spaces from blight or eyesores to amenities is almost guaranteed to boost real estate values in the surrounding area. Adding green space draws new businesses and residences, which in turn spur both economic investment and development money.

Each of these projects comes with a bundle of related urban conditions. Social problems like displacement of existing populations, and affordable housing, layered onto park development, make an already complicated project significantly harder to accomplish. Park projects must confront these related conditions from the very beginning if they hope to have a chance of improving, not exacerbating, inequalities. The balancing act is to make improvements while protecting the people who already live there. The local residents do need to feel like this amenity is also for them. It is not easy, but it is important to do.

Park advocates argue that the projects also come with consequences. Some are positive, like improving how people in a city interact with the space around them, or enabling people to change perspectives, by being elevated 30 feet off the ground, or experiencing innovative technology and sunlight underground. Some are less positive, like driving out small businesses or older residents, or leaving specific communities (families, minorities) out of the design process. Some are both positive and negative, where private money intersects uncomfortably with public space in terms of programming, upkeep, maintenance, and access.

> [These projects] are not only changing the physical form of the cities they're in, they're changing the way we think about those places and what our expectations are for living in them. ...[The park] didn't cause all the problems the city is facing right now, and it can't solve all of them ... it can't be everything. But what it can be is a catalyst for change. (Gravel, quoted in Jacobs 2017)

But, if these 501(c)3 groups can figure out how to enhance a neighborhood's economic viability by adding key amenities while keeping its residents, why is it not been done already? These tasks are critically important for cities. And, these park advocates often have little experience in urban planning.

The High Line's Hammond argues that the act of doing the park projects forces cities to confront their problems:

> I think we [the 501(c)3 groups] have to make the government accountable...you can't just build these [parks] and hope for increased property taxes. You have to look at them holistically. We can't enact zoning. That's the job of the city. But these projects can encourage the city, prod the city, and hold the city accountable. (Hammond, quoted in Jacobs 2017)

The High Line Network, mentioned earlier in Chapter 2, and founded by Hammond, is trying to help new projects think about and manage their own complex balancing acts.

Building green space in cities is tricky; "urban opportunities require a different kind of spatial imagination... If there isn't a park, you have to find someplace that could be a park" (Harnik 2017, via tpl.org). The two successful Friends of the Park groups in New York and Chicago described in this book found an initial theme or combination of themes that reflected an understanding of the site's location, the physical thing, itself, and the realities of actually getting the site built. From the very beginning, FHL and FBT have tried to envision and create parks that would pay homage to the surrounding neighborhoods and their histories. The High Line and 606's successes make doing these projects appealing for city planners and 501c(3) groups.

In New York, at every stage of the process, FHL attempted to preserve and present the history of the High Line. Old railroad tracks were removed, tagged, and (where possible) replaced in the park, so visitors would better understand the story of the railroad. The original Art Deco railings were preserved at great expense. The project's award-winning plant design was inspired by Joel Sternfeld's 2001 photographs of meadows and wildflowers. It may not be quite as wild, messy, or unplanned as we would want, but as a piece of adaptive reuse of transportation infrastructure it is impressive. The team that restored the High Line did so with sensitivity, innovation, and authenticity.

In Chicago, FBT and the Trust for Public Land rightly get much of the credit for involving the community in developing programmatic solutions for the trail. Even getting to the point where work could begin required a complex, cooperative effort between municipal, state and federal agencies, plus private businesses, the police, local communities and residents, who had concerns ranging from access to security to privacy to lighting. The level of neighborhood involvement has been high and sustained.

Where FHL focused on incorporating history into their project, the focus for the 606 in Chicago was on making the trail usable and functional for the community. It is a completely different anchor, but it is one that makes sense in each community. The ability to find that critical anchoring point, one that allows the advocacy group to bootstrap other themes and build a sense of momentum, is not based on economic dominance. Instead, I think it is based on incorporating knowledge of the features and constraints of the situation into discourse themes. That in turn can lead to project progress, new partners, new sources of funding, and so on, which in turn can lead to more success.

When the High Line began construction, the only other park like it in the world was in Paris, and the only U.S.-based efforts to transform railroads into elevated linear parks were underway in New York, Chicago, and Philadelphia. Chicago, Philadelphia, and New York's Lowline have the challenge of managing public expectations in light of the runaway success of the High Line Park. Several other similar reuse projects have been built or gotten underway in Charleston (Grabar 2017), Atlanta (Jacobs 2017), New Orleans, Jersey City, Mexico City, Queens (Randolph 2013), Staten Island (Kensinger 2017), Vancouver, and elsewhere; advocacy groups can choose from two successful models of influencing discourse around their proposed projects.

All of the new groups in other cities are able to point to the High Line and the 606 as examples of what they want to do. But, this is a double-edged sword with both projects. The projects may have affected the discourse and language used to describe and advocate for other projects, even unconsciously. "Advocates would like to see the High Line model take off nationwide in the same way Central Park was copied in the 19th century. But that's a tougher proposition than they think, and it probably won't be worth the effort" (Rybcinski 2012). Not many American cities offer the combination of spatial density and history as New York, and part of the High Line's appeal has been its ability to blend old and new, industrial and green, in unexpected ways. That part of the High Line project is not something that can be easily duplicated.

And, it is extremely unlikely that any of the projects aforementioned will be able to raise the kinds of money FHL did, particularly from private wealthy individuals and corporations, with the possible exceptions of Vancouver and Mexico City. The sources of funding may affect the kinds of discourse themes focused on, as we saw in Chicago, as well as the emphasis on reconciling the themes. In New York, FHL was able to highlight design in their envisioning discourse due to the sheer amount of private money they raised. By contrast, FBT in Chicago focused on the use of the space, because they already knew they would be making design tradeoffs in exchange for initial government funding. The latter decision was a practical choice, and the sense of practicality and pragmatism is prevalent in the FBT discourse. With the High Line and the 606, the 501(3) groups were embedded in networks of resource-integrating, service-exchanging actors coordinating themselves through institutions and institutional arrangements (Vargo and Lusch 2016).

All of these projects are innovative in their approaches to reusing abandoned industrial structures. The issue of finding new public spaces in cities, particularly new green spaces, is not disappearing, and it is not getting any easier. 501(c)3 groups like Friends of the Park groups, or in some cases, business improvement districts, will continue to develop and advocate for these new spaces. Yes, some people do get hurt by these projects. I still think cities should do them, with an eye toward minimizing the downside. As they attempt to appeal to multiple different sources for support, both financial and other, the advocacy groups for these other projects may view the FHL, New York, approach to reconciling competing logics as aspirational, given their own project's constraints. The pragmatic, more limited approach used by FBT in Chicago may be a far more practical choice, though still one that comes with uncomfortable tradeoffs.

Bibliography

Abbott, A. 1990. "Conceptions of Time and Events in Social Science Methods: Causal and Narrative Approaches." *Historical Methods* 23, pp. 140–50.

Abbott, A. 1991. "History and Sociology: The Lost Synthesis." *Social Science History* 15, pp. 201–38.

Abbott, A. 1992. "From Causes to Events: Notes on Narrative Positivism." *Sociological Research and Methods* 20, pp. 428–55.

Abbott, A., and A. Hrycak. 1990. "Measuring Resemblance in Sequence Data: An Optimal Matching Analysis of Musicians' Careers." *American Journal of Sociology* 96, pp. 144–85.

Adams, H. 2016. "The Lowline, NYC's Underground Park, Will Be Replicated Across the World." Retrieved September 2, 2016, from http://forbes.com/sites/henriadams/2016/08/09/the-lowline-nycs-underground-park-will-be-replicated-across-the-world/#1aee9eeb1635

Altshuler, A., and D. Luberoff. 2003. *Mega-projects: The Changing Politics of Urban Public Investment.* New York, NY: Brookings Institution Press.

Amateau, A. November 23, 2005. *Railroad and City Hook Up High Line Transfer Deal.* New York, NY: The Villager.

Amateau, A. January 25, 2006. *Initial Work on High Line park's South End to Begin Next Month.* New York, NY: The Villager.

Bailey, M. October 14, 2011. *Interviewed by M. Plavin.* Tape Recording, via Phone.

Barasch, D. 2016. "The Lowline: A Proposal to Transform the Williamsburg Trolley Terminal into the World's First Underground Park, 154." *The Lowline.* Retrieved from https://issuu.com/thelodown/docs/lowline_proposal_final012816.compre/3?e=14187126/38926963

Barley, S.R., and P.S. Tolbert. 1997. "Institutionalization and Structuration: Studying the Links Between Action and Institution." *Organization Studies* 18, pp. 93–117.

Battilana, J., B. Leca, and E. Boxenbaum. 2009. "How Actors Change Institutions: Towards a Theory of Institutional Entrepreneurship." *Academy of Management Annals* 3, no. 1, pp. 65–107.

Battilana, J., and S. Dorado. 2010. "Building Sustainable Hybrid Organizations: The Case of Commercial Microfinance Organizations." *Harvard Business School,* pp. 1419–40.

Behance Team. 2009. "Robert Hammond: Building the High Line. 99u: Insight on Making Things Happen." Retrieved from http://99u.com/videos/5938/Robert-Hammond-Building-the-High-Line

Benape, A. 2012. *Interviewed by M. Plavin.* Tape Recording, via Phone.

Benford, R.D., and D.A. Snow. 2000. "Framing Processes and Social Movements: An Overview and Assessment." *Annual Review of Sociology* 26, pp. 611–39.

Bjerregaard, T., and J. Lauring. 2012. "Entrepreneurship as Institutional Change: Strategies of Bridging Institutional Contradictions." *European Management Review* 19, pp. 31–43.

Bliss, L. 2017. "The High Line's Biggest Issue—And How Its Creators are Learning from their Mistakes." *The Atlantic*. Retrieved from http://citylab.com/cityfixer/2017/02/the-high-lines-next-balancing-act-fair-and-affordable-development/515391/

Bloom, M., and A. Hauser. July 25, 2017. "606 Bathrooms Finally Coming As Part of $9.4 Million YMCA Expansion." *DNAInfo*.

Bloom, M., and A. Hauser. May 23, 2017. "Anti-gentrification Plan Makes Developers Pay Big For Building Near 606." *DNAInfo*. Retrieved May 24, 2017, from https://dnainfo.com/chicago/20170523/logan-square/606-affordable-housing-ordinance-gentrification-ald-maldonado-ald-moreno

Bornstein, J. October 14, 2011. *Interviewed by M. Plavin*. Tape Recording, via Phone.

Brooks, R. July 25, 2013. "The Lowline, a Fancy Underground Park, Is Pressing the EDC With a Letter Backed by State and Local Pols." *The Village Voice*. Retrieved September 4, 2016, from http://villagevoice.com/news/the-lowline-a-fancy-underground-park-is-pressing-the-edc-with-a-letter-backed-by-state-and-local-pols-6660108

Brush, C.G., T.S. Manolova, and L.F. Edelman. 2008. "Properties of Emerging Organizations: An Empirical Test." *Journal of Business Venturing* 23, no. 5, 547–66. doi:10.1016/j.jbusvent.2007.09.00

Budds, D. October 24, 2016. "The Other High Line Effect: How N.Y.C.'s Glitziest Park Spread Extreme Inequality." *FastCo.Design*. Retrieved from https://fastcodesign.com/3064876/slicker-city/the-other-high-line-effect-how-nycs-glitziest-park-spread-extreme-inequality

Burnley, M. April 5, 2016. "Reading Viaduct Would Make Getting Around Philly Easier." *Phillymag*. Retrieved from http://phillymag.com/citified/2016/04/05/reading-viaduct/

Campbell-Dollaghan, K. 2016. "How NYC's Underground Park Is Piping in Real, Live Sunshine." *Gizmodo.com* .Retrieved September 2, 2016, from http://gizmodo.com/how-nyc-s-underground-park-is-piping-in-real-live-suns-1714662863

Chan, S. 2008. "Lower East Side Is Given 'Endangered' Designation." *The New York Times*. Retrieved from http://nytimes.com/2008/05/21/nyregion/21preserve.html

Ciabotti, J. February 17, 2011. *Interviewed by M. Plavin*. Tape Recording, via Phone.

Cochrane, A. 1999. "Redefining Urban Politics for the Twenty-First Century." In *The Urban Growth Machine: Critical Perspectives Two Decades Later*. Albany, NY: State University of New York Press.

James Corner Field Operations, & Diller Scofidio & Renfro. 2015. *The High Line: James Corner Field Operations, Diller Scofidio & Renfro*. New York, NY: Phaidon Press.

Dailey, J. May 24, 2012. "Chelsea to High Line Tourists: We Pretty Much Hate You." *Curbed*. Retrieved from http://ny.curbed.com/archives/2012/05/24/chelsea_to_high_line_tourists_we_pretty_much_hate_you.php

Danziger, L. June 20, 2011. *Interviewed by M. Plavin*. Tape Recording, via Phone.

Day, A. April 23, 2015. "First look: New York City's Whitney Museum Moves Downtown." *USAToday*. Retrieved June 2, 2017, from https://usatoday.com/story/travel/destinations/2015/04/23/whitney-museum-new-york-city-meatpacking-opening/26246753/

De Monchaux, T. September 22, 2017. "Opinion | How Parks Lose Their Playfulness." *The New York Times*. Retrieved from https://nytimes.com/2017/09/22/opinion/parks-public-spaces-philanthropy.html

Design, A.L.S.L.S. 2015. "Want to Build an Underground Park? You'll Need a Lab First." *Wired.com*. Retrieved September 2, 2016 from https://wired.com/2015/06/want-build-underground-park-youll-need-lab-first/

Dickhut, K. November 14, 2011. *Interviewed by M. Plavin*. Tape Recording, via Phone.

Dickinson, E.E. June 5, 2013. "Lighting the Lowline." *Archlighting.com*. Retrieved September 4, 2016 from http://archlighting.com/projects/lighting-the-lowline_o

DiMaggio, P.J. 1988. "Interest and Agency in Institutional Theory." In *Institutional Patterns and Organizations: Culture and Environment*, ed. L.G. Zucker, 3–21. Cambridge, MA: Ballinger.

DiMaggio, P.J., and W.W. Powell. 1983. "The Iron Cage Revisited: Institutional Isomorphism and Collective Rationality in Organizational Fields." *American Sociological Review*, 48.

Dottor, L. March 17, 2011. *Interviewed by M. Plavin*. Tape Recording, via Phone.

Echevarria, R. May 18, 2011. *Interviewed by M. Plavin*. Tape Recording, via Phone.

Edelstein, D. 2011. *Interviewed by M Plavin*. Notes, via Phone.

Feinstein, L. March 31, 2015. "NYC's Upcoming Subterranean Park Gets A Little Design Help from the Community." Retrieved September 2, 2016 from https://good.is/slideshows/nycs-proposed-underground-park-gets-a-little-design-help-from-the-community

Florida, R. 2003. "Cities and the Creative Class." *City & Community* 2, no. 1, pp. 3–19.

Flyvbjerg, B., N. Bruzelius, and W. Rothengatter. 2003. *Megaprojects and Risk: An Anatomy of Ambition.* Cambridge, UK: Cambridge University Press.

Focht, M. 2011. *Interviewed by M Plavin.* Notes, via Phone.

Franzosi, R. 1998. "Narrative Analysis—Or Why (and How) Sociologists Should Be Interested In Narrative." *Annual Review of Sociology* 24, pp. 517–54.

Friedland, R., and R.R. Alford. 1991. "Bringing Society Back in: Symbols, Practices, and Institutional Contradictions." In *The New Institutionalism in Organizational Analysis,* eds. W.W. Powell and P.J. DiMaggio, 232–66. Chicago, IL: University of Chicago Press.

Fuchs, D. June 5, 2011. *Interviewed by M. Plavin.* Tape Recording, via Phone.

Gartner, W.B. 1985. "A Conceptual Framework for Describing the Phenomenon of New Venture Creation." *The Academy of Management Review* 10, pp. 696–706.

Garud, R., C. Hardy, and S. Maguire. 2007. "Institutional Entrepreneurship as Embedded Agency: An Introduction to the Special Issue." *Organization Studies* 28, no. 7, pp. 957–69.

Gent, C. October 25, 2011. *Interviewed by M. Plavin.* Tape Recording, via Phone.

Glaeser, E.L. 2011. *Triumph of the City : How Our Greatest Invention Makes Us Richer, Smarter, Greener, Healthier, and Happier.* New York, NY: Penguin Press.

Godfrey, A.B.C. 2012. "Bringing Sunlight to Light an Underground Garden." Retrieved September 2, 2016, from http://abcnews.go.com/blogs/technology/2012/12/bringing-sunlight-to-light-an-underground-garden

Gomez-Feliciano, L. June 28, 2011. *Interviewed by M. Plavin.* Tape Recording, via Phone.

Gomez-Feliciano, L. October 20, 2011. *In Person Conversation with M.Plavin, notes.*

Gopnik, A. May 21, 2001. "A Walk on the High Line." *The New Yorker.* Retrieved from http://newyorker.com/magazine/2001/05/21/a-walk-on-the-high-line

Grabar, H. May 9, 2017. "The High Line Conundrum." *Slate.* Retrieved from http://slate.com/articles/business/metropolis/2017/05/can_charleston_emulate_the_high_line_without_deepening_gentrification.html

Greco, L. October, 28, 2011. *Interviewed by M. Plavin.* Notes, in person.

Green, S.E. 2004. "Rhetorical Strategies of Diffusion." *Academy of Management Review* 29, pp. 653–99.

Greenfield, J. May 5, 2017. "Neighbors' Fears of Attracting 'A Different Element' Helped Kill the 606 Skate Park." *ChiStreetsBlog.* Retrieved May 11, 2017, from http://chi.streetsblog.org/2017/05/04/neighbors-fears-of-attracting-a-different-element-helped-kill-the-606-skate-park/

Hammond, R., and J. David. 2007. Hammond and David CNN Interview.

Hammond, R. 2011. Robert Hammond Tedtalk.

Hammond, R. November 12, 2011. *Interviewed by M. Plavin.* Tape Recording, via Phone.

Harnik, P., and B. Welle. 2009. *Measuring the Economic Value of a City Park System,* 30. Trust for Public Land; Center for City Park Excellence.

Hauser, A. April 28, 2017. "Police Give Details On Crime On 606, Call It 'Really Modest'—Logan Square." *DNAinfo.com.*

Hauser, A. July 31, 2017. "Another Cyclist Robbed On 606; Attackers Used Knife To Cut Open His Pockets." *DNAinfo.com.*

Hauser, A. May 19, 2017. "Happy Trails: 606 Use Trending Up 15 Percent." *DNAInfo.com.*

Hauser, A. May 3, 2017. "Controversial Skate Park At East End Of The 606 Scrapped; Neighbors Rejoice." *DNAInfo.com.*

Hauser, A. October 3, 2017. "Cyclist Hits Pedestrian on 606, Leaves Woman Unconscious." *DNAInfo.com.*

Hauser, A. September 25, 2017. "Park District Defends 606 Partial Closure For Fundraiser Dinner Friday." *DNAInfo.com.*

Hawkins, A.J. July 14, 2016. "The Lowline, the World's First Underground Park, Just Cleared a Huge Hurdle." *TheVerge.com.* Retrieved September 2, 2016, from http://theverge.com/2016/7/14/12187632/lowline-underground-park-nyc-lower-east-side-approved

Helphand, B. May 27, 2011. *Interviewed by M. Plavin.* Tape Recording, via Phone.

Hertzberg, A. September 27, 2017. "The 606 Was Blocked Last Friday for a Reason Locals Aren't Happy About." Retrieved October 5, 2017, from http://rare.us/local/chicago/the-606-was-blocked-last-friday-for-a-reason-locals-arent-happy-about/

Hoch, A. 2011. *Interviewed by M Plavin.* Notes, via Phone.

Hu, W. October 7, 2016. "Move Over, Rats: New York Is Planning an Underground Park." *New York Times.* Retrieved from http://nytimes.com/2016/10/08/nyregion/move-over-rats-new-york-is-planning-an-underground-park.html

Institute for Housing Studies—DePaul University. 2017. "Cook County House Price Index: Fourth Quarter 2016." Retrieved from https://housingstudies.org/data/ihs-price-index/cook-county-house-price-index-fourth-quarter-2016/

Jacobs, J. 1961. *The Death and Life of Great American Cities.* New York, NY: Vintage Books.

Jacobs, K. October 16, 2017. "The High Line Network Tackles Gentrification." *Architect Magazine.* Retrieved from http://architectmagazine.com/design/the-high-line-network-tackles-gentrification_o

Jenkins, J.C. 1983. "Resource Mobilization Theory and the Study of Social Movements." *Annual Review of Sociology* 9, pp. 527–53.

Jonas, A., and D. Wilson. 1999. "The City as A Growth Machine." In *The Urban Growth Machine: Critical Perspectives Two Decades Later*. Albany, NY: State University of New York Press.

Katz, J., and W.B. Gartner. 1988. "Properties of Emerging Organizations." *The Academy of Management Review* 13, pp. 429–41.

Kensinger, N. May 4, 2017. "Could this Abandoned Staten Island Railway Become the Next High Line?" *Curbed.com* Retrieved May 11, 2017, from https://ny.curbed.com/2017/5/4/15536752/staten-island-north-shore-railway-photo-essay

Kopp, J. October 13, 2017. "Four Features of Philly's Upcoming Rail Park | PhillyVoice." Retrieved October 14, 2017, from http://phillyvoice.com/four-features-phillys-upcoming-rail-park/

Kress, G., and T. Van Leeuwen. 2001. *Multimodal Discourse: The Modes and Media of Contemporary Communication*. Edward Arnold.

Lange, A. August 15, 2016. "Stop Calling the Lowline a Park." *Curbed NY*. Retrieved from http://ny.curbed.com/2016/8/15/12404404/lowline-new-york-park

Lawrence, T.B., and R. Suddaby. 2006. "Institutions and Institutional Work." In *Handbook of Organization Studies*, eds. S. Clegg, C. Hardy and W. Nord. London, UK: Sage.

Leca, B., J. Battilana, and E. Boxenbaum. 2008. *Agency and Institutions: A Review of Institutional Entrepreneurship*. Working Paper, 08-096.

Leopold, D. November 23, 2011. *Interviewed by M. Plavin*. Tape Recording, via Phone.

Levere, M. December 2014. *The High Line Park and Timing of Capitalization of Public Goods*. San Diego, CA: University of California.

Levy, P. April 2011. *Interviewed by M. Plavin*. Notes, in person.

Ling, M.P.E. 2013. "High Line Architecture." *Cargocollective.com*. Retrieved September 2, 2016, from http://cargocollective.com/Uofanycstudioarch/HIGH-LINE-ARCHITECTURE

Lounsbury, M. 2007. "A Tale of Two Cities: Competing Logics and Practice Variation in the Professionalizing of Mutual Funds." *Academy of Management Journal* 50, pp. 289–307.

Lounsbury, M., and E. Boxenbaum. 2013. "Institutional Logics in Action, Part A." *Research in the Sociology of Organizations* 39A, pp. 3–22.

Maguire, S., and C. Hardy. 2006. "The Emergence of New Global Institutions: A Discursive Perspective." *Organization Studies* 27, no. 1, pp. 7–29.

Marquis, C., and M. Lounsbury. 2007. "Vive la Résistance: Competing Logics and the Consolidation of U.S. Community Banking." *Academy of Management Journal* 50, pp. 799–820.

Matarrita-Cascante, D., R. Stedman, and A.E. Luloff. 2010. "Permanent and Seasonal Residents' Community Attachment in Natural Amenity-Rich Areas: Exploring the Contribution of Landscape-Related Factors." *Environment and Behavior* 42, no. 2, pp. 197–220.

McAdam, D., J.D. McCarthy, and M.N. Zald. 1988. "Social Movements." In *Handbook of Sociology*, ed. N. Smelser, 695–737. Newbury Park, CA: Sage Publications.

McCann, E.J. 2002. "The Cultural Politics of Local Economic Development; Meaning-Making, Place-Making, and the Urban Policy Process." *Geoforum* 33, pp. 385–98.

McCarthy, C. October 24, 2017. "Here's What Designers Have In Mind for the Underground Park on the Lower East Side." *Patch*. Retrieved from https://patch.com/new-york/lower-east-side-chinatown/heres-what-designers-have-mind-underground-park-lower-east-side

McEneaney, S. 2011. *Interviewed by M Plavin*. Notes, in person.

McGraw Hill Construction. April 1, 2003. "Design News: High Line Design Competition." *New York Construction*. Retrieved from http://thehighline.org/press/articles/040103_nyconstruction/

Meyer, R.E., I. Egger-Peitler, M.A. Hollerer, and G. Hammerschmid. 2013. "Of Bureaucrats and Passionate Public Managers: Institutional Logics, Executive Identities, and Public Service Motivation." *Public Administration*. Published online April 18, 2013.

Morgan, R. December 26, 2012. "Neighborhood Boost Seen from the Lowline." *Wall Street Journal (Online)*. Retrieved from http://search.proquest.com/docview/1243275216?accountid=29121

Oberg, E. February 24, 2011. *Interviewed by M. Plavin*. Tape Recording, via Phone.

Ostrom E. September 1, 2008. "Institutions and the Environment." *Economic Affairs* 28, no. 3, pp. 24–31.

Pache, A.-C., and F. Santos. 2010. "Inside the Hybrid Organization: An organizational Level View of Responses to Conflicting Institutional Demands." *Research Center ESSEC Working Paper*, 11001.

Perry-Smith, J.E., and P.V. Mannucci. 2015. "Social Networks, Creativity, and Entrepreneurship." In *The Oxford Handbook of Creativity, Innovation, and Entrepreneurship*, eds. C.C. Shalley, M.A. Hitt, and J. Zhou. New York, NY: Oxford University Press.

Perry-Smith, J.E., and P.V. Mannucci. 2017. "From Creativity to Innovation: The Social Network Drivers of the Four Phases of the Idea Journey." *Academy Of Management Review* 42, no. 1, 53–79. doi:10.5465/amr.2014.0462

Peter, H. March 31, 2011. *Interviewed by M. Plavin*. Tape Recording, via Phone.

Phillips, N., T.B. Lawrence, and C. Hardy. 2004. "Discourse and Institutions." *Academy of Management Review* 29, no. 4, pp. 635–52.

Plavin-Masterman, M. 2013. *Making the Imagined Real: How Institutional Entrepreneurs Transform Public Space*, Scholars Press, an imprint of AV Akademikerverlag GmbH & Co. KG, Heinrich-Boecking Str. 6-8 D 66121 Saarbrücken.

Polletta, F. 1998. "Contending Stories: Narrative in Social Movements." *Qualitative Sociology* 21, no. 4, pp. 419–46.

Popkin, N. October 18, 2013. "Official 'Marriage' of Reading Viaduct Advocates | Hidden City Philadelphia." *Hidden City Philadelphia*. Retrieved from http://hiddencityphila.org/2013/10/official-marriage-of-reading-viaduct-advocates/

Prahalad, D. 2011. *Interview by M. Plavin*. Skype.

Prahalad, D., and R. Sawhney. 2011. *Predictable Magic: Unleash the Power of Design Strategy to Transform Your Business*. Pearson Education, Publishing as Wharton School Publishing.

Quintana, M. August 2016. "Changing Grid: Exploring the Impact of the High Line." *StreetEasy*. Retrieved from http://streeteasy.com/blog/changing-grid-high-line/

Quirk, V. October 2015. "The Lowdown on the Lowline, the World's First Underground Park." *Atlas Osbscura*. Retrieved September 2, 2016, from http://atlasobscura.com/articles/the-lowdown-on-the-lowline-the-worlds-first-underground-park

Rafter, C. July 2015. "Lowline Kickstarter Campaign Raises $200,000." *Observer*. Retrieved September 2, 2016, from http://observer.com/2015/07/lowline-kickstarter-campaign-raises-200000/

Rao, H., C. Morrill, and M. Zald. 2000. " Power Plays: How Social Movements and Collective Action Create New Organizational Forms." *Research in Organizational Behavior* 22, pp. 237–81.

Reay, T., and C.R. Hinings. 2009. "Managing the Rivalry of Competing Institutional Logics." *Organization Studies* 30, no. 6, pp. 629–52.

Riverlife. 2015. *Three Rivers Park Economic Impact Analysis*. Pittsburgh.

Robinson, G. December 16, 2005. "This Train is Bound for Glory." *NY Blade*. Retrieved from http://thehighline.org/press/articles/121605_nyblade/

Romero, M. August 31, 2016. "Here's the Story Behind those 'Have You Seen this Park?' signs around Philly." *Curbed Philly*. Retrieved May 8, 2017, from https://philly.curbed.com/2016/8/31/12715382/reading-viaduct-rail-park-ad-campaign

Romero, M. March 9, 2017. "See the winning Rail Park Tunnel designs for the Better Philadelphia Challenge." Retrieved August 30, 2017, from https://philly.curbed.com/2017/3/9/14867464/rail-park-tunnel-renderings-better-philadelphia-challenge

Romero, M. September 1, 2017. "Rail Park Hits Construction Milestone with First Concrete Pour." Retrieved September 13, 2017 from https://philly. curbed.com/2017/9/1/16240598/philadelphia-rail-park-construction-concrete-pour

Sassatelli, R. March 2009. "A Serial Ethnographer: An Interview with Gary Alan Fine." *Qualitative Sociology* 33, no. 1, pp. 79–96.

Satow, J. May 18, 2012. *Amanda Burden Wants to Remake New York: She Has 19 Months Left.* New York, NY: New York Times.

Saz-Carranza, A., and F. Longo. 2012. "Managing Competing Institutional Logics in Public-Private Joint Ventures." *Public Management Review* 14, no. 3, pp. 331–57.

Schoonhoven, C.B., and E. Romanelli. 2001. "Emergent Themes and the Next Waves of Entrepreneurship Research." *In the Entrepreneurship Dynamic: Origins of Entrepreneurship and the Evolution of Industries,* 383–440. Palo Alto, CA: Stanford University Press.

Schreiber, K. March 2011. *Interviewed by M. Plavin.* Notes, in person.

Scott, W.R. 2001. *Institutions and Organizations,* 2nd ed., chapters 2–4, 6. Thousand Oaks, CA: Sage Publications.

Scott, W.R. 2004. "Reflections on a Half-Century of Organizational Sociology." *Annual Review of Sociology* 30, pp. 1–21.

Scott, W.R. 2008. "Approaching Adulthood: The Maturing of Institutional Theory." *Theory and Society* 37, no. 5, p. 427.

Spunt, D. May 19, 2017. "Old Reading Railroad Line to Become Walking Trail." *CBS Philly.* Retrieved May 21, 2017, from http://philadelphia.cbslocal. com/2017/05/19/reading-railroad-line-trail/

Stein, P. May 11, 2011. *Interviewed by M. Plavin.* Tape Recording, via Phone.

Stone, A. 2012. *Interviewed by M. Plavin.* Tape Recording, via Phone.

Suchman, M.C. 1995. "Managing Legitimacy: Strategic and Institutional Approaches." *Academy of Management Review* 20, no. 3, pp. 571–610.

Suddaby, R., and R. Greenwood. 2005. "Rhetorical Strategies of Legitimacy." *Administrative Science Quarterly* 50, no. 1, pp. 35–67.

Surana, K. 2015. "Community Board Balks as City Moves to Activate 'Lowline Site.'" *Bedford and Bowery.com.* Retrieved from http://bedfordandbowery. com/2015/12/community-board-balks-as-city-moves-to-activate-lowline-site/

Sweeting, K. 2015. "Digging the Lowline." *The Awl.* Retrieved September 2, 2016, from https://theawl.com/digging-the-lowline-5fc25ebe67f4#.stp zm81xv

Tanenbaum, M. May 3, 2017. "Heineken Sponsors Crowdfunding Campaign for Philadelphia Rail Park." *PhillyVoice.* Retrieved May 4, 2017, from http:// phillyvoice.com/heineken-launches-crowdfunding-campaign-philadelphia-rail-park/

Tavernise, S. May 31, 2012. "A Gap in College Graduates Leaves Some Cities Behind." *New York Times*. Retrieved from http://nytimes.com/2012/05/31/us/as-college-graduates-cluster-some-cities-are-left-behind.html?pagewanted=1&_r=1&ref=general&src=me

The Lo-Down. 2011. "The Lowline: A Conversation with the Delancey Underground Team." *The Lo-Down : News from the Lower East Side*. Retrieved September 2, 2016, from http://thelodownny.com/leslog/2011/09/a-conversation-with-the-low-line-team.html#

The Lo-Down. 2013. "LowLine Team Returns to CB3, Addresses Gentrification, Funding Questions." *The Lo-Down: News from the Lower East Side*. Retrieved September 4, 2016, from http://thelodownny.com/leslog/2013/02/lowline-team-returns-to-cb3-addresses-gentrification-funding-questions.html#

The Lo-Down. 2014. "Lowline Update: Tech Lab Receives City Funding, Young Designers Show Off Ideas." *The Lo-Down : News from the Lower East Side*. Retrieved September 2, 2016, from http://thelodownny.com/leslog/2014/07/lowline-update-tech-lab-receives-city-funding-young-designers-show-off-ideas.html?utm_source=feedburner&utm_medium=twitter&utm_campaign=Feed%3A+feedburner%2FhxHq+%28The+Lo-Down%29#

Thornton, P.H., and W. Ocasio. 2008. "Institutional Logics." *The Sage Handbook of Organizational Institutionalism*, 99–128. Thousand Oaks, CA: Sage Publications.

Tracey, P., N. Phillips, and O. Jarvis. 2011. "Bridging Institutional Entrepreneurship and the Creation of New Organizational Forms: A Multilevel Model." *Organization Science* 22, no. 1, pp. 60–80.

Tracy, S., and K. Lyons. January 1, 2013. "Service Systems and the Social Enterprise." *Human Factors and Ergonomics in Manufacturing & Service Industries* 23, no. 1, pp. 28–36.

Urbanski, M. April 27, 2011. *Interviewed by M. Plavin*. Tape Recording, via Phone.

Urek, A. 2011. *Interviewed by M Plavin*. Notes via Phone.

Vargo, S., and R.F. Lusch. January 2004. "Evolving to a New Dominant Logic for Marketing." *Journal of Marketing* 68, no. 1, pp. 1–17.

Vargo, S., and R.F. Lusch. January 2016. "Institutions and Axioms: An Extension and Update of Service-dominant Logic." *Journal of the Academy of Marketing Science* 44, no. 1, pp. 5–23.

Vargo, S., and R.F. Lusch. March 2008. "Service-dominant Logic: Continuing the Evolution." *Journal of the Academy of Marketing Science* 36, no. 1, pp. 25–38.

von Furstenberg, D. 2011. *Diane von Furstenberg interview with Charlie Rose*. Transcribed.

Wood, L.A., and R.O. Kroger. 2000. *Doing Discourse Analysis: Methods for Studying Action in Talk and Text*. Thousand Oaks, CA: Sage Publications.

Yanow, D. 2005. "How [sic] Built Spaces Mean: A Semiotics of Space." In *Interpretation and Method: Empirical Research Methods and the Interpretive Turn*. Armonk, NY: M.E. Sharpe.

Zilber, T.B. July 2007. "Stories and the Discursive Dynamics of Institutional Entrepreneurship: The Case of Israeli High-tech After the Bubble." *Organization Studies* 28, pp. 1035–54.

About the Author

Miriam Plavin-Masterman is an assistant professor in Worcester State University's Business Administration and Economics Department. She received a BSc in Industrial/Labor Relations from Cornell University, an MBA from Dartmouth College's Amos Tuck School of Business Administration, and an MA, and PhD in Sociology from Brown University. She studies the efforts of entrepreneurs to reclaim abandoned spaces in support of making cities more livable. More specifically, she examines the discourse practices entrepreneurs engage in that help them sustain their projects over the long time periods in which they occur (often 10 years or more). In doing so, her research contributes to a better understanding of how these projects come to be, what impacts they have on the cities they are in, and other, later projects trying to emulate their success.

Index

OTHER TITLES IN OUR SERVICE SYSTEMS AND INNOVATIONS IN BUSINESS AND SOCIETY COLLECTION

Jim Spohrer, IBM and Haluk Demirkan, Arizona State University, Editors

- *Citizen-Centered Cities, Volume I: Case Studies of Public Involvement* by Paul R. Messinger
- *Citizen-Centered Cities, Volume II: City Studies of Public Involvement* by Paul R. Messinger
- *Fair Pay: Adaptively Win-Win Customer Relationships* by Richard Reisman
- *Collaborative Innovation: How Clients and Service Providers Can Work By Design to Achieve It* by Tony Morgan
- *Service Design with Applications to Health Care Institutions* by Oscar Barros
- *How Can Digital Technologies Improve Public Services and Governance?* by Nagy K. Hanna
- *The Accelerating TechnOnomic Medium ('ATOM'): It's Time to Upgrade the Economy* by Kartik Gada
- *Sustainability and the City: The Service Approach* by Adi Wolfson

Announcing the Business Expert Press Digital Library

Concise e-books business students need for classroom and research

This book can also be purchased in an e-book collection by your library as

- a one-time purchase,
- that is owned forever,
- allows for simultaneous readers,
- has no restrictions on printing, and
- can be downloaded as PDFs from within the library community.

Our digital library collections are a great solution to beat the rising cost of textbooks. E-books can be loaded into their course management systems or onto students' e-book readers.
The **Business Expert Press** digital libraries are very affordable, with no obligation to buy in future years. For more information, please visit **www.businessexpertpress.com/librarians**. To set up a trial in the United States, please email **sales@businessexpertpress.com**.

www.ingramcontent.com/pod-product-compliance
Lightning Source LLC
Chambersburg PA
CBHW071837200326
41519CB00016B/4141